Catholic Christianity

for Edexcel
Revision Guide

Victor W. Watton

Catholic Christianity

for Edexcel Revision Guide

THIRD EDITION

Photo credit: p.96 Rvin88.

Orders: please contact Bookpoint Ltd, 130 Milton Park, Abingdon, Oxon OX14 4SB. Telephone: (44) 01235 827720. Fax: (44) 01235 400454. Lines are open 9.00–5.00, Monday to Saturday, with a 24-hour message answering service. Visit our website at www.hoddereducation.co.uk

© Victor W. Watton 2003
First published in 2003 by
Hodder & Stoughton Limited,
An Hachette UK Company
338 Euston Road
London NW1 3BH

Second Edition published in 2007.
This Third Edition published in 2010.

Impression number   8
Year   2014

Cover photos *l–r*: © Giulio Napolitano/AFP/Getty Images; © Reuters/Corbis; © Royal Observatory, Edinburgh/AATB/Science Photo Library
Typeset in 12/14pt Electra LH Regular by Gray Publishing, Tunbridge Wells.
Printed and bound in India

A catalogue record for this title is available from the British Library.

ISBN: 978 0340 975 558

Contents

SECTION 10.1 **BELIEFS AND VALUES**

SECTION 10.2 **COMMUNITY AND TRADITION**

SECTION 10.3 **WORSHIP AND CELEBRATION**

SECTION 10.4 **LIVING THE CHRISTIAN LIFE**

APPENDIX 1

APPENDIX 2

Introduction

This book is designed to support your revision of the Edexcel GCSE Religious Studies Specification: Unit 3 Religion and Life based on the study of Roman Catholic Christianity and Unit 10 Roman Catholic Christianity.

Each section of the book covers one of the four sections of each Unit. Each section begins with a list of the key words you need to learn. Then each sub-topic within the specification for that section is covered as a separate topic. Each topic:

- has a summary of the key points
- outlines the main points needed to answer the explain questions (question c)
- gives arguments for and against the issues raised by the topic to make it easier to answer the response questions (question b) and the evaluation questions (question d).

Each section finishes with guidance on how to answer exam questions and an end of section test.

The book also contains an appendix to give you guidance on self-marking the end of section tests and how to improve your performance on the section tests.

How to use the book

1 Learn a section at a time.
2 Learn the key words of a section.
3 Work through each topic in a section in this way:
   - learn the key points of the topic
   - learn the main points
   - learn the advice on how to answer evaluation questions.
4 When you have learned all eleven topics, do the end of section test.
5 Use the mark scheme from Appendix 1 to mark your test, and go through the guidance on how to improve your performance. If you find it difficult to self-mark the test, visit www.hoddereducation.co.uk/catholicchristianity where there is a more specific mark scheme for each test.
6 Make sure you know everything in Appendix 2 before you take the examination.

Section 3.1 **Believing in God**

KEY WORDS FOR SECTION 3.1	
Agnosticism	not being sure whether God exists
Atheism	believing that God does not exist
Conversion	when your life is changed by giving yourself to God
Free will	the idea that human beings are free to make their own choices
Miracle	something which seems to break a law of science and makes you think only God could have done it
Moral evil	actions done by humans which cause suffering
Natural evil	things which cause suffering but have nothing to do with humans
Numinous	the feeling of the presence of something greater than you
Omni-benevolent	the belief that God is all-good
Omnipotent	the belief that God is all-powerful
Omniscient	the belief that God knows everything that has happened and everything that is going to happen
Prayer	an attempt to contact God, usually through words

Topic 3.1.1 The main features of a Catholic upbringing and how it may lead to belief in God

Main points

The main features of a Catholic upbringing

Catholic parents are likely to:

- have their babies baptised and promise to bring up their children to believe in God and be good Catholics
- teach their children to believe in God
- teach their children to pray to God
- take their children to Mass where they learn to worship God
- send their children to a Catholic school.

How a Catholic upbringing may lead to, or support, belief in God

It is natural for children who have had a Catholic upbringing to believe in God because:

- Their Catholic parents will have told them about God and they will believe their parents.
- Catholics pray to God, so they will believe that God exists because their parents would not waste their time praying to nothing.
- Seeing so many people worshipping God when they go to Mass will make them believe that God exists.
- They will be taught that God exists when they go to school, and will believe it because their teachers tell them it is true.

Evaluation questions

You may be required to argue for and against having a Catholic upbringing.

1. People who think a Catholic upbringing is a good thing, may use these arguments:
   - A Catholic upbringing helps to keep a family together as parents and children join together for Catholic activities.
   - A Catholic upbringing gives children an understanding of what is right and wrong, and gives them good morals.
   - A Catholic upbringing gives children a sense of belonging and community, giving them emotional stability.

2. People who think a Catholic upbringing is a bad thing, may use these arguments:
   - A Catholic upbringing means children are brought up following a religion they have not chosen themselves.
   - Some people think that a Catholic upbringing can take away a child's human right to freedom of religion.
   - A Catholic upbringing may work against community cohesion by making Catholic children think followers of other religions are wrong.

Topic 3.1.2 How religious experience may lead to belief in God

Key points

- Religious experience is something which makes people feel God's presence.
- People experience God in the numinous, conversion, miracles and answered prayers.
- Religious experience makes people feel that God is real, and so they believe he must exist.

Main points

Religious believers who have had a religious experience will find that the experience makes their belief in God stronger because they believe they have had direct contact with God.

The numinous is a feeling of the presence of God. When people are in a religious building, in a beautiful place or looking up at the stars on a clear night, they may be filled with the awareness that there is something greater than them, which they feel to be God. Such a feeling is likely to lead them to believe in God.

Conversion is used to describe an experience of God, which is so great that people experiencing it want to change their lives or religion and commit themselves to God in a special way. Conversion experiences make people believe in God because they feel that God is calling them to do something for him.

A miracle is an event that breaks a law of science and can only be explained by God. If you experience something that seems to break all the laws of science, you will look for an explanation, and if the only explanation you can think of is a miracle, you will start believing in God.

Religious believers think they can make contact with God through prayer. If the person praying feels that God is listening to the prayer, then they are likely to believe that God exists. Also, an answered prayer (for example, when someone prays for a sick loved one to recover and they do) will lead to belief in God.

Evaluation questions

You may be required to argue for and against religious experience proving God's existence.

1. People who think religious experience proves God's existence may use the arguments in the main points above.
2. People who think religious experience does not prove God's existence may use these arguments:
   - A numinous experience is caused by your surroundings, whether a church or the stars, and may have nothing to do with God.
   - All miracles can be explained. For example, Jesus may not have been dead when he was taken down from the cross and so he just recovered rather than rising from the dead.
   - There are more unanswered prayers than answered ones, so they surely prove God does not exist.

Topic 3.1.3 The argument from design and belief in God

Main points

Design means making a plan to produce something. For example, a car is made to the plan of the designer, and looking at any part of the car makes you think that the car has been designed.

Many religious believers have looked at the world and seen that the way the universe works makes it look as if it has been designed. Some scientists also see evidence of design in the process of evolution where complex life-forms develop from simple ones. From this they have developed the argument from design:

- Anything that has been designed needs a designer.
- There is plenty of evidence that the world has been designed (laws of science such as gravity and magnetism; DNA being a blueprint for life, etc.).
- If the world has been designed, the world must have a designer.
- The only possible designer of something as wonderful as the universe would be God.
- Therefore the appearance of design in the world proves that God exists.

This argument supports belief in God and may lead those who are not sure to believe there is a God.

Key points

- The universe seems to be designed.
- Anything that is designed must have a designer.
- God must therefore exist because only God could have designed the universe.

Evaluation questions

You may be required to argue for and against the design argument.

1. People who think the design argument proves God's existence may use the arguments in the bullet list in the main points above.
2. People who think the argument from design does not prove God exists may use these arguments:
   - No designer would have created things like volcanoes, earthquakes, etc.
   - Science can explain the appearance of design without needing God.
   - The argument does not explain how things like dinosaurs could have been part of a design plan for the world.
   - Even if the argument worked, it would only prove that the universe has a designer, not that this designer is God.

Topic 3.1.4 The argument from causation and belief in God

Key points

- The way everything seems to have a cause makes people think the universe must have a cause.
- The only possible cause of the universe is God.
- So God must exist.

Main points

Causation is the process of one thing causing another. For example, a driver pressing the brake pedal causes the effect of the car slowing down.

The argument from causation

- Cause and effect seem to be a basic feature of the world. Whatever we do has an effect. If I do my homework (cause), I will please my parents and/or teachers (effect). Modern science has developed through looking at causes and effects, and scientific investigations seem to show that any effect has a cause and any cause has an effect.
- This means that the universe, the world and humans must have had a cause.
- God is the only logical cause of the universe.
- Therefore God must exist.

Evaluation questions

You may be required to argue for and against the argument from causation.

1. People who think the argument from causation proves God's existence may use these arguments:
   - The argument makes sense of ourselves and the universe because it explains how and why we are here.
   - The argument fits in with our common sense. We cannot believe that something can come from nothing and the argument shows that everything came from God.
   - The argument fits in with science which tells us that every effect has a cause and so the universe (an effect) must have a cause (God).
   - We believe that things must have started off, they must have a beginning or First Cause; and the argument explains that God started off the universe.

2. People who think the argument from causation does not prove God's existence may use these arguments:
   - If everything needs a cause then God must need a cause. Why should the process stop with God?
   - It is possible that matter itself is eternal and so was never created. That would mean that the process of causes could go back for ever.
   - Just because everything in the universe needs an explanation does not mean the universe needs an explanation. The universe could just have been there for ever.
   - Even if there was a First Cause it would not have to be the God of any particular religion. It could be good, evil, a mixture of good and evil, several gods, etc.

Topic 3.1.5 Scientific explanations of the world and agnosticism and atheism

Main points

Science explains how the world came into being in this way:

- Matter is eternal.
- About 15 billion years ago, the matter of the universe exploded. This is known as the Big Bang theory. The red shift in light from other galaxies is evidence that the universe is still expanding.
- As the matter of the universe flew away from the explosion, it formed stars and then our solar system.
- The gases on the Earth's surface produced primitive life.
- The genetic structure of these primitive life-forms led to the evolution of new life-forms and, about 2.5 million years ago, humans evolved. (The evidence of fossils shows new life-forms coming into existence and genetic research shows the similarities of life-forms, for example 50 per cent of human DNA is the same as that of a cabbage.)

How the scientific explanation of the world may lead to agnosticism or atheism

If science can explain the universe and humans without God, it can lead some people to be agnostic, as they no longer need God to explain why we are here.

Other people may become atheists because they believe that if God existed, he must have made the world and be the only explanation for it. So the way that science can explain the world and humans without God is proof to such people that God does not exist.

Key points

Science says that matter is eternal and that the universe began when this matter exploded. The solar system came out of the explosion, and the nature of the Earth allowed life to develop through evolution.

Evaluation questions

Advice on answering evaluation questions is after Topic 3.1.6 on page 8.

Topic 3.1.6 How Catholics respond to scientific explanations of the world

Key points

- Many Catholics accept the scientific explanations but believe they show that God created the universe through the Big Bang.
- Some Catholics believe that both science and the Bible are true because one of God's days could be billions of years.

Main points

There are two Catholic responses to scientific explanations of the world.

Response one

Many Catholics accept that the scientific explanations are true, but they believe that the scientific explanations prove that God created the universe because they believe:

- Only God could have made the Big Bang at exactly the right microsecond to form the universe.
- Only God could have made laws such as gravity which the matter of the Big Bang needed to form solar systems.
- Only God could have made the gases on Earth react in such a way to form life.

Response two

Some Catholics believe that both the scientific explanations and the Bible are correct. They claim that the main points of the Bible's story of creation fit with science, but one of God's days could be millions or billions of years.

Evaluation questions

You may be required to argue for and against the scientific explanations of the world proving God does not exist.

1. People who think the scientific explanations prove that God does not exist are likely to use such arguments as:
   - If God existed, he would be the only explanation of the world. Therefore the fact that science can explain the world and humans without God is proof that God does not exist.
   - The Big Bang was an accident and there is no evidence that it was caused by God.
   - An omnipotent and omniscient God would not have created the world in such a wasteful way with species developing and dying out over billions of years just so humans could arrive.

2. You should use the arguments in Catholic response one above to argue against this.

Topic 3.1.7 Why unanswered prayers may lead to agnosticism or atheism

Main points

If people say their prayers in church and at home, but never feel the presence of God when they pray, they may feel there is no God listening to them. The feeling that no one is listening to their prayers leads them to agnosticism, or even atheism.

Unanswered prayers are even more likely to lead people to believe God does not exist. Religious people believe that God answers people's prayers, and they often hear about people's prayers being answered. If their prayers to God are not answered, they may feel that God does not like them, or that God does not exist.

If someone has been a good Catholic (going to Mass on Sundays and holy days and living a good life following the teachings of the Church), but when they pray for God to cure their sick child, their child dies, that person may lose their faith in God.

If someone's prayers are not answered, particularly if they are praying for something like the end of human suffering in wars, droughts, etc., then they might stop believing in God. This is because they may think God could not exist if he lets such things continue to happen. In this way, unanswered prayers can lead a person to become an agnostic or an atheist.

Key points

If people do not feel God's presence when they pray, or if people pray for good things, but their prayers are not answered, they may start to doubt God's existence. If God does not answer prayers, how do you know he exists?

Evaluation questions

Advice on answering evaluation questions is after Topic 3.1.8 on page 10.

Topic 3.1.8 How Catholics respond to unanswered prayers

Key points

Catholics believe that God cannot answer selfish prayers. But he answers all other prayers, although not always in the way people expect, because his answers have to fit in with his overall plans.

Main points

Most Catholics believe that God answers all prayers and that what seems to be unanswered prayers can be explained by the following:

- If you pray for selfish things, like God allowing you to pass an exam without any work, God will let you fail so that you work hard next time.
- Your prayer may not be answered in the way you expect because God has different plans, for example he may want an ill person to enter heaven.
- Just like a human parent, God may answer our prayers by giving us what we need rather than what we have asked for.
- Catholics believe that God loves people and so they believe God's love will answer their prayers in the best possible way, even though it may not look like a direct answer.
- Catholics have faith that God will answer all prayers in the best way for the person praying, or the people prayed for, even if it is different from what they expected.

Evaluation questions

You may be asked to argue for and against unanswered prayers proving that God does not exist.

1. People who believe unanswered prayers prove that God does not exist are likely to use such arguments as:
   - Christians believe that God is their loving heavenly Father who will answer their prayers, so if he does not answer them, he cannot exist.
   - Christians are told about answered prayers. For example, people being cured of terminal cancer by prayer, but far more people have their prayers unanswered. A good God would not answer a few prayers for a cure and not answer lots of prayers for a cure. Therefore it is unlikely that God exists.
   - If there was a God, he would answer the prayers of good religious people, and there would be no wars, no starvation, etc. The prayers of such people are clearly not answered, so God cannot exist.

2. Catholic Christians would argue that unanswered prayers do not disprove God's existence, using the arguments in the main points above.

Topic 3.1.9 Why evil and suffering may lead to agnosticism or atheism

Main points

Evil and suffering can take two forms:

- Moral evil is caused by humans using their free will. Wars and crimes such as rape, murder and burglary are good examples of moral evil.
- Natural evil is suffering that has not been caused by humans. Earthquakes, floods, volcanoes, cancers and so on are not caused by humans, but they result in lots of human suffering.

How evil and suffering cause people to question or reject belief in God

Philosophers express the problem in this way:

- If God is omnipotent (all-powerful), he must be able to remove evil and suffering from the world.
- If God is omni-benevolent (all-good), he must want to remove evil and suffering from the world.
- It follows that, if God exists, there should be no evil or suffering in the world.
- As there is evil and suffering in the world, either God is not all-good and powerful or he does not exist.

Also, if God knows everything (omniscient), he must have known the evil and suffering that would come from creating the universe. So he should have created the universe in a way that avoided evil and suffering.

Most religious believers believe that God is omnipotent, omni-benevolent and omniscient. So the existence of evil and suffering challenges their beliefs about God.

For many religious believers, evil and suffering become a problem if they experience it (for example, they are in an earthquake, or their child dies from a disease), when it can change them into an atheist or an agnostic.

Key points

Some people do not believe in God because they think that there would be no evil and suffering in a world created by a good and powerful God. A good God should not want such things to happen, and a powerful God ought to be able to get rid of them but does not.

Evaluation questions

Advice on answering evaluation questions is after Topic 3.1.10 on page 13.

Topic 3.1.10 How Catholics respond to the problem of evil and suffering

Key points

Catholics respond to the problem of evil and suffering by:

- praying for those who suffer
- helping those who suffer
- claiming that evil and suffering are the fault of humans misusing their free will
- claiming that evil and suffering are part of a test to prepare people for heaven
- claiming that God has a reason for allowing evil and suffering, but humans are too limited to understand it.

Main points

Catholics respond to the problem of evil and suffering in several ways. Most Catholics would use at least two responses to explain how an all-good, all-powerful God can allow evil and suffering.

Response one

Many Catholics believe from the Bible that God must have a reason for allowing evil and suffering, but humans cannot understand it, so the correct response of Catholics is to follow the example of Jesus and fight against evil and suffering as Jesus did by praying for those who suffer and by helping those who suffer.

Many Catholics become doctors, nurses, social workers, etc. to help to reduce the amount of suffering in the world.

Response two

Many Catholics claim that, by giving humans free will, God created a world in which evil and suffering will come about through humans misusing their free will. So evil and suffering is a problem caused by humans, not God.

Response three

Many Catholics believe that the evil and suffering involved in this life are not a problem, because this life is a preparation for paradise. If people are to improve their souls, they need to face evil and suffering in order to become good, kind and loving. God cannot remove evil and suffering if he is going to give people the chance to become good people. But, in the end, he will show his omni-benevolence and omnipotence by rewarding the good in heaven.

Response four

Some Catholics claim that God has a reason for not using his power to remove evil and suffering, but humans cannot understand it. God is divine and there is no way humans can understand his thoughts.

Evaluation questions

You may be asked to argue for and against evil and suffering proving that God does not exist.

1. People who believe evil and suffering prove that God does not exist are likely to use such arguments as:
   - If God is omnipotent, he must be able to remove evil and suffering from the world. If God is omni-benevolent, he must want to remove evil and suffering from the world. It follows that, if God exists, there should be no evil or suffering in the world. As there is evil and suffering in the world, God does not exist.
   - A good God would not have designed a world with floods, earthquakes, volcanoes, cancers, etc. These cannot be blamed on humans and so they are evidence that God did not make the world and so does not exist.
   - An all-powerful God would not allow evil humans like Hitler and Stalin to cause so much suffering, so as individual humans have caused lots of suffering, God cannot exist.

2. Catholic Christians believe evil and suffering do not disprove God's existence using the arguments in responses one, two and three on page 12.

Topic 3.1.11 How two programmes about religion may affect a person's attitude to belief in God

Key points

You need to study two programmes or films about religion. For each one you will need to know:

- an outline of its contents
- how it might have encouraged some people to believe in God
- how it might have encouraged some people not to believe in God
- whether it affected your beliefs about God.

Main points

You have to study two programmes or films about religion in depth and work out how they could affect a person's attitude to belief in God.

From your class notes you should have:

- A summary of each programme.
- Four pieces of evidence from each programme to show how it might have encouraged some people to believe in God.
- Four pieces of evidence from each programme to show how it might have encouraged some people not to believe in God.
- What effect the programme had on your own attitude to belief in God and four reasons for this.

Evaluation questions

You may be asked to argue for and against programmes or films about religion affecting belief in God.

1. To show that programmes or films do affect beliefs about God, you should:

Either

- Use four pieces of evidence from a programme to show how it might have encouraged some people to believe in God.

Or

- Give four reasons why the programme affected your own attitude to belief in God.

2. To show how programmes or films do not affect beliefs about God, you should:

Either

- Use four pieces of evidence from a programme to show how it might have encouraged some people not to believe in God.

Or

- Give four reasons why the programme affected your own attitude to belief in God.

How to answer questions on Section 3.1

The a) question – key words

These questions give you up to two marks just for knowing the key words and their meanings. This means you must learn the key words because you can gain ten per cent of the marks if you get the a) questions right.

Have a look at the following examples.

Question
What is moral evil? (2 marks)

> Up to four marks will be awarded for your spelling, punctuation and grammar in your answer to Section 3.1 of the exam paper. This means you should take extra care with your spelling and make sure you use full stops and capital letters. You should use paragraphs if your answers to parts c) and/or d) are long.
> Four marks for spelling, punctuation and grammar can move an A to an A*, a B to an A, etc., remember to take extra care with your spelling and punctuation to answers in Section 3.1.

Answer
Actions done by humans which cause suffering.

> Two marks for a correct definition.

Question
What name is given to people who believe there is no God? (2 marks)

Answer
Atheist

> Two marks for a correct definition.

The b) question – what do you think?

These questions give you up to four marks for giving your own opinion about one of the issues, but you will only gain marks if you give reasons for your opinion.

You must decide what you think about the issues and ideas you study. The questions are meant to be quite easy and to get full marks you just need to give two developed reasons. They are really like part (i) of an evaluation question (question d) where you have to give two reasons. So, to answer a response question, you could use two of the reasons from the point of view you agree with in the evaluation questions advice for each topic. The following example shows you what is meant by developed reasons.

Question
Do you think miracles prove that God exists? Give TWO reasons for your point of view. (4 marks)

Answer
Yes, I do think miracles prove God exists because they are in the Bible.

> One mark for a reason.

For example, Jesus rose from the dead which has to be a miracle.

> Two marks because the reason is developed.

Also, miracles still happen today.

> Three marks for a second reason.

For example, many people are cured today when they are taken to Lourdes.

> Four marks because the second reason is developed.

> Total = four marks.

The c) question – explain

You can gain two marks for giving a brief reason in basic English even if the spelling and grammar are poor. You will also only get two marks if you describe the issue rather than trying to explain it.

You can gain four marks by giving two brief reasons with a limited command of English and little use of specialist vocabulary.

You can gain five marks by giving three brief reasons, but this will rise to six marks if it is written in a clear style of English with some use of specialist vocabulary.

You can gain seven marks by using four brief reasons, but this will rise to eight marks if you write in a clear and correct style of English with a correct use of specialist vocabulary where appropriate.

Explain questions are where your Quality of Written Communication is tested, so you should answer these questions in a formal style of English, be careful with your spelling and try to use some specialist vocabulary. You can gain four extra marks on the paper if your written English is good, which could move an A to an A*, a B to an A, etc.

Have a look at the following example.

Question

Explain why unanswered prayers may cause problems for religious believers. (8 marks)

Answer

LEVEL 1: two marks for a reason expressed in basic English.	If people say their prayers in church and at home, but never feel the presence of God when they pray, they may feel there is no God listening to them.
LEVEL 2: by developing the reason, the answer goes up to level 2 and because the answer is written in clear English it would gain four marks.	Religious people believe that God answers people's prayers, and they often hear about people's prayers being answered. If their prayers to God are not answered, they may feel that God does not like them, or that God does not exist.
LEVEL 3: by adding another reason the answer moves up to level 3 and because the answer is written in a clear style of English with some use of specialist vocabulary (presence of God, religious people, Catholic, Mass, teachings of the Church) it would gain six marks.	If someone has been a good Catholic (going to Mass on Sundays and holy days and living a good life following the teachings of the Church), but when they pray for God to cure their sick child, their child dies, that person may lose their faith in God.
LEVEL 4: by adding a further reason, the answer moves up to level 4 and because it is written in a clear and correct style of English with extra specialist vocabulary (agnostic, atheist, human suffering) it would gain eight marks – full marks.	If someone's prayers are not answered, particularly if they are praying for something like the end of human suffering in wars, droughts, etc., then they might stop believing in God. This is because they may think God could not exist if he lets such things continue to happen. In this way, unanswered prayers can lead a person to become an agnostic or an atheist.

The d) question – evaluation

To answer these questions you need to decide what you think about the quotation and then give three reasons for why you think that.

Then you need to give three reasons why some people (for example, Catholics if you are an atheist, or atheists if you are a Catholic) would disagree with you.

One of your points of view should always be religious so that you can give religious reasons.

Have a look at the following example.

Question
'The Argument from Causation proves that God exists.'

(i) Do you agree? Give reasons for your opinion. (3 marks)
(ii) Give reasons why some people may disagree with you. (3 marks)

Answer

(i) I do agree because the universe must have been caused by someone.

Science tells us that every effect has a cause. The universe is an effect and so it must have a cause.

The only possible cause of the universe is God so he must exist. So I think this argument proves that God exists.

(ii) I can see why some people would disagree with me because they think that if everything needs a cause then God must need a cause; why should the process stop with God?

They may also think that it is possible that matter itself is eternal and so was never created. That would mean that the process of causes could go back for ever.

Finally, they may argue that just because everything in the universe needs an explanation does not mean the universe needs an explanation. The universe could just have been there for ever.

One mark for a personal opinion with a reason.

The reason is developed so it moves up to two marks.

The answer now develops to a conclusion referring to the question, so it moves up to three marks.

One mark for a reason why some people might disagree.

Another reason is given so it moves up to two marks.

The answer now gives another reason for some people disagreeing, so it moves up to three marks.

This answer to question d) can gain full marks because although both parts refer to religious reasons, the question did not ask for reference to Christianity.

SECTION 3.1 TEST

SECTION 3.1: Believing in God

Answer both questions.

1. a) What is natural evil? (2 marks)

   b) Do you think scientific explanations of the world show that God does not exist? Give two reasons for your point of view. (4 marks)

   c) Explain why the design argument leads some people to believe in God. (8 marks)

   d) 'Answered prayers prove that God exists.'

      (i) Do you agree? Give reasons for your opinion. (3 marks)

      (ii) Give reasons why some people may disagree with you. (3 marks)

   (Total: 20 marks)

2. a) What is free will? (2 marks)

   b) Do you think that programmes or films about religion can affect a person's beliefs about God? Give two reasons for your point of view. (4 marks)

   c) Explain why religious experience may lead some people to believe in God. (8 marks)

   d) 'There is no evidence that God exists.'

      (i) Do you agree? Give reasons for your opinion. (3 marks)

      (ii) Give reasons why some people may disagree with you. (3 marks)

   In your answer you should refer to Christianity.

   (Total: 20 marks)

You should now use the mark scheme in Appendix 1, page 135, to mark your answers, and the self-help tables in Appendix 1, pages 136–137, to see how you can improve your performance. If you need more help with the mark scheme for these questions, go to www.hoddereducation.co.uk/catholicchristianity

Section 3.2 Matters of life and death

KEY WORDS FOR SECTION 3.2

Abortion	the removal of a foetus from the womb before it can survive
Assisted suicide	providing a seriously ill person with the means to commit suicide
Euthanasia	the painless killing of someone dying from a painful disease
Immortality of the soul	the idea that the soul lives on after the death of the body
Near-death experience	when someone about to die has an out of body experience
Non-voluntary euthanasia	ending someone's life painlessly when they are unable to ask, but you have good reason for thinking they would want you to do so
Paranormal	unexplained things which are thought to have spiritual causes, e.g. ghosts, mediums
Quality of life	the idea that life must have some benefits for it to be worth living
Reincarnation	the belief that, after death, souls are reborn in a new body
Resurrection	the belief that, after death, the body stays in the grave until the end of the world when it is raised
Sanctity of life	the belief that life is holy and belongs to God
Voluntary euthanasia	ending life painlessly when someone in great pain asks for death

Topic 3.2.1 Why Catholics believe in life after death and how this affects their lives

Key points

Catholics believe in life after death because:

- Jesus rose from the dead
- the Bible and the creeds say there is life after death
- the Church teaches that there is life after death
- the soul is something that can never die.

Their beliefs about life after death affect their lives because Catholics will try to love God and love their neighbour so that they go to heaven and not purgatory or hell.

Evaluation questions

You may be asked to argue for and against Catholic beliefs in life after death. For arguments for belief in life after death see 'Why Catholics believe in life after death' on this page and for arguments against life after death see Topic 3.2.3, page 22.

Main points

Why Catholics believe in life after death

- The main Christian belief is that Jesus rose from the dead as this is what is recorded in the Gospels and New Testament. This proves there is life after death.
- St Paul teaches that people will have a resurrection like that of Jesus.
- The major creeds of the Church teach that Jesus rose from the dead and that there will be life after death.
- The Catechism of the Catholic Church teaches that there is life after death. The Catechism contains the teaching of the Magisterium, which all Catholics should believe.
- Many Catholics believe in life after death because it gives their lives meaning and purpose.

How beliefs about life after death affect the lives of Catholics

- Many Catholics believe that only if they have lived a good Catholic life will they be allowed into heaven. So they try to live a good Catholic life following the teachings of the Church so that they go to heaven when they die.
- Living a good Catholic life means following the two greatest commandments – love of God and love of neighbour. So Catholics' lives will be affected as they try to love God by praying and attending Mass every Sunday.
- In the Parable of the Sheep and Goats Jesus said Catholics should feed the hungry, clothe the naked, befriend strangers and visit the sick and those in prison. Jesus taught in the Good Samaritan that loving your neighbour means helping anyone in need. These teachings are bound to affect Catholics' lives and explain why some Catholics work for charities such as CAFOD, SVP, etc.
- Catholics believe that sin prevents people from going to heaven, and those who die with unforgiven sins will go to purgatory to be purified. Therefore Catholics will try to avoid committing sins in their lives so that they will go to heaven.

Topic 3.2.2 Non-religious reasons for believing in life after death

Main points

There are three main parts of the paranormal that provide non-religious reasons for believing in life after death.

1 Near-death experiences

This is when someone is clinically dead for a time and then comes back to life, and can remember what happened. Research by doctors in Britain, Holland and the USA has shown that about eight per cent of these cases have a near-death experience. The main features of these experiences are: feelings of peace; floating above the body; seeing a bright light; entering a heavenly place where they see dead relatives. If near-death experiences are true, there must be life after death.

2 Evidence for a spirit world

Many people think of ghosts and ouija boards as evidence for a spirit world, but the clearest evidence comes from mediums. A medium is a person who claims to be able to communicate between our material world and a spirit world where the spirits of the dead live.

There are mediums in all countries and in all religions. They feature frequently on television channels such as Living TV. Most mediums claim that religious leaders like Jesus and Muhammad were in touch with the spirit world. They claim the spirit world gives people a second chance at life. Mediums contact people's dead relatives giving information they would not be able to without their contact being true. If mediums can contact the dead, there must be life after death.

3 The evidence of reincarnation

Hindus, Sikhs and Buddhists believe in reincarnation and have collected much evidence for this happening. If reincarnation is true, then there is life after death.

Evaluation questions

You may be asked to argue for and against the non-religious reasons for believing in life after death.

1. To argue for, you should use the reasons above.

2. To argue against, you could use these reasons:
   - Near-death experiences have been challenged by most scientists who claim they are simply products of the patient's brain as a result of chemical changes. Therefore there is no life after death.
   - The evidence from mediums is also very suspect. Many mediums have been proven to be frauds. The only fool-proof test for mediums being true (set by Robert Thouless) has never been passed by a medium. So they do not prove there is life after death.
   - Most beliefs about life after death think that the mind or soul can survive without the body, but science shows that the mind cannot live without the brain, so when the body dies, the mind must also die.

Topic 3.2.3 Why some people do not believe in life after death

Main points

Some people do not believe in God and believe this life is all there is. They do not believe in life after death because:

- If there is no God, there is no spirit world for life after death to happen.
- The different religions contradict each other about life after death. Christianity, Islam and Judaism say it will be resurrection or immortality of the soul; Hinduism, Sikhism and Buddhism say it will be reincarnation. If life after death were true, they would all say the same thing.
- Much of the evidence is based on holy books, but they contradict each other, and there is no way of deciding which holy books are true and which false.
- The evidence of the paranormal (near-death experiences, mediums, reincarnation) has all been challenged by scientists.
- Most beliefs about life after death think that the mind or soul can survive without the body, but science shows that the mind cannot live without the brain, so when the body dies, the mind must also die.
- There is no place where life after death could take place; space journeys have shown heaven is not above the sky.
- People who have been brought up by atheists will not believe in life after death.

Evaluation questions

You may be asked to argue for and against there being a life after death, using evidence from at least one religion.

1. To argue for there being life after death, you should use the reasons why Catholics believe in life after death (see Topic 3.2.1, page 20).

2. To argue against, you should use the reasons in the main points above.

Topic 3.2.4 The nature of abortion

Main points
1967 Act

The law says that abortion is only allowed if two doctors agree:

- the mother's life is at risk
- the mother's physical or mental health is at risk
- the child is very likely to be born severely handicapped
- there would be a serious effect on other children in the family.

1990 Act

Abortions cannot be carried out after 24 weeks of pregnancy, unless the mother's life is at risk, or the foetus has severe handicaps.

Why abortion is a controversial issue

Abortion is a controversial issue because:

- Many people believe that life begins at the moment of conception. Therefore abortion is taking a human life.
- Many people believe that life begins when the foetus is able to live outside the mother. Therefore abortion is not taking life.
- Many non-religious people believe that a woman should have the right to do what she wants with her own body. They might argue that an unwanted foetus is no different from an unwanted tumour.
- Many religious people believe that the unborn child's right to life is greater than the mother's rights.
- Some people argue the time limit should be reduced to 18 or 20 weeks because of medical advances.
- There are also arguments about whether medical staff should have to carry out abortions.

Key points

Abortion is allowed in the United Kingdom if two doctors agree that there is medical reason for it.

Abortion is a controversial issue because:

- people disagree about when life begins
- people disagree about whether abortion is murder
- people disagree about whether a woman has the right to choose.

Evaluation questions

Any evaluation questions are likely to ask you to refer to Christianity, so the advice on evaluation questions is after Topic 3.2.5 on page 24.

Topic 3.2.5 Different Christian attitudes to abortion

Key points

Christians have different attitudes to abortion:

- Some Christians believe that abortion is always wrong because it is murder and against God's will.
- Some Christians believe that abortion is wrong but must be allowed in some circumstances as the lesser of two evils.

Main points

Christians have two differing attitudes to abortion:

1 The Catholic Church teaches that all abortion is wrong whatever the circumstances (apart from medical treatments for the mother which affect the life of the foetus). They believe this because:

- Life belongs to God, so only God has the right to end a pregnancy.
- Life begins at conception so abortion is taking life and this is banned in the Ten Commandments.
- They should follow the teaching of the Catechism that all abortion is murder.
- Counselling, help and adoption are alternatives to abortion for women made pregnant as a result of rape so that good can come out of evil in a new life.

2 Other Christians (mainly Liberal Protestants) disagree with abortion, but think it must be allowed in certain circumstances because they believe that:

- Life does not begin at conception.
- Jesus' command to love your neighbour means it is the duty of Christians to remove suffering, which abortion does.
- The sanctity of life can be broken in such things as a just war, so why not in a just abortion (for example when the mother's life is at risk)?
- If doctors have developed tests for certain medical conditions in unborn babies, parents should be allowed abortions if such tests show their baby would be born with serious medical problems.

Evaluation questions

You are likely to be asked one of two types of evaluation question about abortion.

1. One type will say something like: 'No Christian should ever have an abortion.' To answer this type of question you would use the reasons why some Christians think abortion is always wrong to argue for (part 1 of the main points above); and the reasons why some Christians allow abortion to argue against (part 2 of the main points above).

2. The other type will say something like: 'Every woman should have the right to an abortion if she wants one.' People who agree with this would use such reasons as:
   - Life does not begin at conception, it begins when the foetus is capable of surviving outside the

womb on its own, so abortion is not the same as murder.
- Abortion prevents a great deal of suffering. If babies are brought into the world with mothers who do not want them and cannot afford to bring them up, the babies will suffer, the mothers will suffer, and society will suffer in dealing with the situation.
- A woman should have the right to do what she wants with her own body. They might argue that an unwanted foetus is no different from an unwanted tumour.

To argue against, you should use the Catholic reasons against abortion from part 1 of the main points above.

Topic 3.2.6 The nature of euthanasia

Main points

Euthanasia is normally thought of as providing a gentle and easy death to someone suffering from a painful, deadly disease and who has little quality of life. This can be done by: assisted suicide, voluntary euthanasia, non–voluntary euthanasia.

British law says that all these methods of euthanasia are murder. However, the law now agrees that stopping artificial feeding or not giving treatment (often called passive euthanasia), are not euthanasia and so are lawful.

Why euthanasia is a controversial issue

1 Many people want euthanasia to remain illegal because:
   • There is always likely to be doubt as to whether it is what the person really wants.
   • There is also the problem as to whether the disease will end the life; a cure might be found for the disease.
   • It is the job of doctors to save lives, not end them. Would patients trust doctors who kill their patients?
   • People might change their mind, but then it would be too late.
   • Who would check that it was only people who really wanted and needed euthanasia who died?

2 Many people want euthanasia to be made legal because:
   • Discoveries in medicine mean that people who would have died are being kept alive, often in agony, and should have the right to die.
   • Doctors have the right to switch off life-support machines if they think the patient has no chance of recovering, and allow people who have been in a coma for years to die. So euthanasia is already legal.
   • People have a right to commit suicide, so why not give them the right to ask doctors to assist their suicide if they are too weak to do it alone?
   • Just as doctors can now switch off life-support machines, so judges have said that doctors can stop treatment.

Key points

There are various types of euthanasia that are all aimed at giving an easy death to those suffering intolerably. British law says that euthanasia is a crime, but withholding treatment from dying patients is not.

Euthanasia is a controversial issue because:

• medicine can keep people alive with little quality of life
• suicide is no longer a crime
• we give euthanasia to suffering animals
• the role of doctors is to save life not kill
• can you ever be sure that euthanasia is what someone wants?

Evaluation questions

You may be asked to argue for and against the law on euthanasia being changed (this means euthanasia becoming legal).

1. The arguments for euthanasia becoming legal would come from part 2 in the main points above.

2. The arguments against would come from part 1 in the main points above.

Topic 3.2.7 Christian attitudes to euthanasia

Main points

Although all Christians believe that euthanasia is wrong, there are slightly different attitudes:

1 Catholics (and many Liberal Protestants) believe that assisted suicide, voluntary euthanasia and non-voluntary euthanasia are all wrong. However, they believe that switching off life-support machines, not giving treatment that could cause distress, and giving dying people painkillers which may shorten their life are not euthanasia. They have this attitude because:

- They believe in the sanctity of life. Life is created by God and so it is up to God, not humans, when people die.
- They regard euthanasia as murder, which is forbidden in the Ten Commandments.
- If doctors say someone is brain-dead, then they have already died, so switching off the machine is accepting what God has already decided.
- If you give painkillers to a dying person in great pain, and they kill the person, this is not murder because your intention was to remove their pain, not to kill them (doctrine of double effect).

2 Some Christians believe any form of euthanasia is wrong including switching off life-support machines, the refusal of extraordinary treatment, or the giving of large doses of painkillers. They have this attitude because:

- They take the Bible teachings literally and the Bible forbids suicide.
- Euthanasia includes switching off life-support machines, the refusal of extraordinary treatment, and giving large doses of painkillers because life is being ended by humans not God.
- All forms of euthanasia are murder, which is banned by the Ten Commandments.
- They believe that life is sacred and should only be taken by God. The Bible says that life and death decisions belong to God alone.

3 A few Christians accept euthanasia in certain circumstances because:

- Medical advances mean it is hard to know what God's wishes about someone's death are. God may want someone to die but doctors are keeping them alive.
- The teaching of Jesus on loving your neighbour can be used to justify assisting suicide, because it might be the most loving thing to do.
- It is a basic human right to have control over your body and what people do to it. People have a right to refuse medical treatment, so why not a right to ask for euthanasia.

Evaluation questions

You may be asked to argue for and against euthanasia referring to Christianity.

1. The arguments for euthanasia should come from part 2 of the main points in Topic 3.2.6 (page 25) and also from part 3 in the main points on the right.

2. The arguments against could be the reasons why Christians are against euthanasia given in parts 1 and 2 in the main points above.

Topic 3.2.8 The media and matters of life and death

Main points

The media are all forms of communication, including newspapers, television, radio, films and the internet. Remember that the word is plural.

1 Arguments that the media should not be free to criticise what religions say about matters of life and death

- Some people believe that criticising what religions say on matters of life and death is a way of stirring up religious hatred, which is banned by the Racial and Religious Hatred Act of 2007.
- Many religious believers believe the freedom of the media should be limited because of the offence criticism of religious attitudes can bring. For example, when a Danish newspaper published cartoons of the Prophet Muhammad in 2006, there were riots in some countries.
- Some religious believers believe that criticising what religious leaders say about matters of life and death is close to the crime of blasphemy.
- Some religious people feel that religious statements are based on what God says and so are beyond human criticism.

2 Arguments that the media should be free to criticise what religions say about matters of life and death

- Freedom of expression is a basic human right which is needed for democracy to work. Before people vote they need to know what is going on in the world and in their own country. For this they need free media, and if the media have freedom of expression, then they must be free to criticise religious attitudes on matters of life and death.
- If religious leaders use the media to make statements about matters of life and death (as they do on things like stem-cell research), they must be prepared for the media to criticise those statements.
- In a multi-faith society, there must be freedom of religious belief and expression, so the media must have the right to question and even criticise not only religious beliefs, but also what religions say about life and death issues.
- Life and death issues are so important to everyone that people want to know what is the right view. This would be difficult if religions were allowed to put forward views that no one could criticise.

Key points

Some people think that what religions say about matters of life and death should not be criticised by the media because:
- they might stir up religious hatred
- they might be offensive to religious believers.

Other people think the media should be free to criticise religious attitudes because:
- a free media is a key part of democracy
- if religions want to be free to say what they want, then the media must be free to criticise religion.

Evaluation questions

You may be asked to argue for and against the media being free to criticise religious attitudes to matters of life and death.

1. For arguments for the media being free to criticise you should use the arguments in part 2 in the main points on the left.

2. For arguments against the media being free to criticise you should use the arguments in part 1 in the main points on the left.

Topic 3.2.9 How an issue from matters of life and death has been presented in one form of the media

Key points

When studying the presentation of an issue from matters of life and death in the media, you must be able to explain:

- why the issue was chosen
- how it was presented
- whether the presentation treated religious beliefs fairly
- whether the presentation treated religious people fairly.

Main points

You have to study how *one* issue from matters of life and death has been presented in *one* form of the media.

From your class notes you should have:

- Notes on why the issue is important and why you think the producers decided to focus on this issue.
- An outline of how the issue was presented, listing the main events and the way the events explored the issue.
- Notes on the way religious beliefs are treated in the presentation of the issue.
- Four pieces of evidence on whether you think the presentation was fair to religious beliefs.
- Four pieces of evidence on whether you think the presentation was fair to religious people.

Evaluation questions

Although you are unlikely to be asked an evaluation question on this topic, if you were, it would be about whether the media treat religious beliefs or people fairly.

1. To argue that media are fair, you should use:
   - The evidence you have from one form of the media for the religious beliefs being treated fairly.
   - The evidence you have from one form of the media for religious people being treated fairly.

2. To argue that media are not fair, you should use:
   - The evidence you have from one form of the media for the religious beliefs not being treated fairly.
   - The evidence you have from one form of the media for religious people not being treated fairly.

Topic 3.2.10 The causes of world poverty

Main points

The main causes of world poverty are listed below.

Natural disasters

Many LEDCs (less economically developed countries) are situated in areas of the world where natural disasters (earthquakes, floods, droughts, etc.) can destroy many thousands of homes and the farmland on which the people depend.

Debt

Most LEDCs have to borrow money from the banks of developed countries to survive and begin to develop. However, the amount of interest they have to pay can actually make the countries poorer.

Wars

Many LEDCs have been badly affected by wars (often caused by the effects of colonialism). Wars destroy crops, homes, schools, hospitals, and so on, causing even more poverty. They also force many people to leave their homes and become refugees in other safer countries. These neighbouring countries may have been developing, but the sudden arrival of refugees with no money or food can make that country poor again.

Unfair trade

World trade is controlled by the rich countries of the world who decide the prices paid for products from LEDCs. For example, the rich countries pay grants to their own farmers to grow crops, and put high taxes on imported crops from LEDCs so those products are more expensive.

HIV/AIDS

This disease is killing many people in LEDCs. The loss of so many earners and the growing numbers of orphans are causing many poor countries to become poorer.

Other factors

There are other causes of world poverty. Lack of education means that young people in LEDCs have few or no skills. Lack of clean, fresh water leads to disease, short life expectancy and large families (so some children will survive to look after their parents).

Key points

The main causes of world poverty are:

- natural disasters
- wars
- debt
- unfair trade
- lack of education
- HIV/AIDS.

Evaluation questions

Any evaluation questions on world poverty are likely to ask you to refer to Christianity or Catholic Christianity, so the advice on evaluation questions is given after Topic 3.2.11 on page 31.

Topic 3.2.11 How and why CAFOD is trying to remove the causes of world poverty

Key points

CAFOD works for world development by:

- promoting long-term development schemes
- responding to emergencies
- raising public awareness of the causes of poverty
- speaking out on behalf of poor communities.

It works to end world poverty because:

- Jesus taught that Christians should help the poor
- the Catholic Church teaches that Catholics should help the poor
- they believe it is the way to follow the Golden Rule.

Main points

How CAFOD is trying to end world poverty

Development programmes

CAFOD works with partner groups in LEDCs to promote development in such ways as:

- opening clinics and training health workers
- helping to give street children an education so that they can earn a living
- helping to set up savings schemes and different farming projects so that subsistence farmers are not wiped out by natural disasters.

Disasters and emergencies

CAFOD has a disaster fund to deal with natural disasters and refugees. CAFOD has sent food, antibiotics and shelters to victims of the tsunami and supplies to war refugees in Bosnia, Kosovo and Rwanda.

Raising awareness

About five per cent of CAFOD's budget is spent on educating the people and churches of England and Wales about the need for development and how Catholics can help. It publishes a newspaper called *Friday* and many educational materials.

Speaking out on behalf of poor communities to bring social justice

CAFOD was heavily involved in the Make Poverty History campaign of 2005, the largest ever world campaign to end poverty, and is now involved in the Trade Justice Campaign to change the rules of world trade so that poor countries can work themselves out of poverty.

Why CAFOD is trying to end world poverty

- According to the New Testament, riches must be used for the help of others, especially the poor.
- Jesus told the Parable of the Sheep and the Goats where he said that feeding the hungry and clothing the naked is like feeding and clothing Jesus himself. Catholics want to help Jesus and so they help the poor and suffering.
- The parable also teaches that helping the poor is the way to heaven, and Catholics want to get to heaven.
- In the Sermon on the Mount, Jesus taught that Christians should share their time and money to help the poor.
- The Catholic Church teaches that Christians have a duty to help the poor and suffering, as Pope Benedict showed in his first encyclical.
- The Golden Rule for Christians is to treat other people in the way you would like to be treated, and everyone would want to be helped if they were starving.

Evaluation questions

1. You may be asked to argue for and against world poverty being caused by selfishness, greed or lack of religion.
   - To argue for, you could use the examples of debt, unfair trade and wars, and for each one explain how it could be caused by selfishness or greed or not following the teachings of religion. For example, unfair trade is caused by rich nations being selfish and wanting to protect their own producers and also by their greed to make more money at the expense of poor nations.
   - To argue against, you could use the examples of natural disasters, HIV/AIDS and wars (some wars are caused by religion) and explain how each is not caused by selfishness, greed or lack of religion. For example, earthquakes cause lots of poor nations to become poorer, but no one could argue that earthquakes are caused by human greed or selfishness or by ignoring religion.

2. You may be asked to argue for and against religion being the best way to end world poverty.
   - To argue for you could use the reasons why CAFOD is trying to end world poverty in the main points above.
   - To argue against you could use the examples of debt, unfair trade, wars and natural disasters and explain how each would be better solved by government or UN action than by religion because it needs governments to provide lots of money and work together whatever the religion.

How to answer questions on Section 3.2

You should already know the basics about how to answer examination questions from Section 3.1, pages 15–17, but here is an answer to a whole question on Section 3.2 with a commentary to help you.

Question a)
What is resurrection? (2 marks)

Answer
Coming back to life.

> One mark for a partially correct answer.

Answer
The belief that, after death, the body stays in the grave until the end of the world when it is raised.

> Two marks for a correct definition.

Question b)
Do you think euthanasia should be allowed?
Give TWO reasons for your point of view. (4 marks)

Answer
I do not think euthanasia should be allowed because euthanasia is murder …

> One mark for a reason.

… which is banned in the Bible and the teachings of the Church.

> Two marks because the reason is developed.

Also, Christianity teaches that all life is sacred …

> Three marks because a second reason is given.

… and so life should only be taken by God because life belongs to God.

> Four marks because the second reason is developed.

> Total = four marks.

Question c)
Explain why some Christians allow abortion and some do not. (8 marks)

Answer
Liberal Protestants disagree with abortion, but think it must be allowed in certain circumstances because they believe that life does not begin at conception.

> LEVEL 1: two marks for a reason for one attitude expressed in basic English.

They also believe that Jesus' command to love your neighbour means it is the duty of Christians to remove suffering, which abortion does.

> LEVEL 2: by giving a second reason for the attitude, the answer goes up to level 2 and because the answer is written in clear English it would gain four marks.

Catholic Christians believe that all abortion is wrong whatever the circumstances because they believe that life begins at conception so abortion is taking life and this is banned in the Ten Commandments.

> LEVEL 3: by adding another attitude with a reason the answer moves up to level 3 and because the answer is written in a clear style of English with some use of specialist vocabulary (Liberal Protestant, conception, command, Catholic, banned, Ten Commandments) it would gain six marks.

The Catechism of the Catholic Church says that all abortion is murder, and Catholics should follow the teaching of the Catechism because it is the teaching of the Magisterium decided by the Pope and Bishops.

> LEVEL 4: By adding a further reason for the second attitude, the answer moves up to level 4 and because it is written in a clear and correct style of English with extra specialist vocabulary (Catechism, Magisterium, Pope, Bishops) it would gain eight marks – full marks.

Question d)

'There is no evidence for life after death.'

(i) Do you agree? Give reasons for your opinion.   (3 marks)
(ii) Give reasons why some people may disagree with you.   (3 marks)

In your answer, you should refer to Catholic Christianity.

Answer

(i) I disagree because I am a Catholic and I believe that Jesus rising from the dead proves there is life after death.

> One mark for a personal opinion with a reason.

The Bible and the Church teach that there is life after death, and I believe that both the Bible and the Church come from God and so must be true.

> Another reason is given so it moves up to two marks.

I also think there must be a life after death to make sense of this life. There must be a life after death in which people will be judged on how they have lived this life so that the good are rewarded and the evil are punished, and this is what God promises in the teaching of the Church about heaven, hell and purgatory.

> The answer now gives another reason for the opinion, so it moves up to three marks.

(ii) Atheists would disagree with me because they believe there is no God, and if there is no God, there can be no life after death.

> One mark for a reason why some people might disagree.

They also think that most beliefs about life after death are based on the mind or soul surviving without the body, but science shows that the mind cannot live without the brain, so when the body dies, the mind must also die.

> Another reason is given so it moves up to two marks.

They also believe that there is no place where life after death could take place; space journeys have shown heaven is not above the sky. If there is nowhere for life after death to take place, there cannot be a life after death.

> The answer now gives another reason for some people disagreeing, so it moves up to three marks.

> This answer to question d) can gain full marks because part (i) refers to Catholic Christianity.

SECTION 3.2 TEST

SECTION 3.2: Matters of life and death

Answer both questions.

1. a) What is quality of life? (2 marks)

   b) Do you think there is life after death?
      Give two reasons for your point of view. (4 marks)

   c) Explain how their beliefs about life after death affect the lives of Christians. (8 marks)

   d) 'Religious people should never have abortions.'

      (i) Do you agree? Give reasons for your opinion. (3 marks)

      (ii) Give reasons why some people may disagree with you. (3 marks)

      In your answer, you should refer to Christianity.

   (Total: 20 marks)

2. a) What is immortality of the soul? (2 marks)

   b) Do you think the media should be free to criticise what religion says about matters of life and death? Give two reasons for your point of view. (4 marks)

   c) Explain why Catholic Christians believe in life after death. (8 marks)

   d) 'Everyone should have the right to euthanasia if they have no quality of life.'

      (i) Do you agree? Give reasons for your opinion. (3 marks)

      (ii) Give reasons why some people may disagree with you. (3 marks)

      In your answer you should refer to Christianity.

   (Total: 20 marks)

You should now use the mark scheme in Appendix 1, page 135, to mark your answers, and the self-help tables in Appendix 1, pages 136–137, to see how you can improve your performance. If you need more help with the mark scheme for these questions, go to www.hoddereducation.co.uk/catholicchristianity

Section 3.3 Marriage and the family

KEY WORDS FOR SECTION 3.3

Adultery	a sexual act between a married person and someone other than their marriage partner
Civil partnership	a legal ceremony giving a homosexual couple the same legal rights as a husband and wife
Cohabitation	living together without being married
Contraception	intentionally preventing pregnancy from occurring
Faithfulness	staying with your marriage partner and having sex only with them
Homosexuality	sexual attraction to the same sex
Nuclear family	mother, father and children living as a unit
Pre-marital sex	sex before marriage
Procreation	making a new life
Promiscuity	having sex with a number of partners without commitment
Re-constituted family	where two sets of children (stepbrothers and stepsisters) become one family when their divorced parents marry each other
Re-marriage	marrying again after being divorced from a previous marriage

Topic 3.3.1 Changing attitudes to marriage, divorce, family life and homosexuality in the UK

Key points

- Fifty years ago, most people only had sex in marriage, and they married in church. Now, people have sex before they marry, cohabiting is socially acceptable and most marriages are not in church. This could be caused by safer contraception and fewer people being influenced by religion.
- Divorce and re-marriage used to be rare but are accepted today, and two in five marriages end in divorce. The changes may have been caused by cheaper divorce and women having more equality.
- Family life has changed so that, although most children are still brought up by a mother and a father, the parents may not be married or they may have been married more than once. These changes are probably caused by the changing attitudes to sex, marriage and divorce.
- Homosexuality used to be illegal, but now homosexuals have the same rights to sexual activity as heterosexuals, including civil partnerships. These changes are probably due to discoveries showing homosexuality is natural, and changes to the law.

Main points

In the UK in the 1960s, it was expected that young people only had sex after marriage; most married young, in church, for life; families were husband and wife and children (nuclear family); and male homosexuality was a criminal offence.

How attitudes have changed

- Most people have sex before marriage.
- Many couples live together (cohabit) rather than marry.
- The average age for marrying has increased.
- Most marriages do not take place in church.
- Divorce is accepted as a normal part of life.
- There is much more divorce and so more single-parent families and re-constituted families.
- There are more extended families as more mothers are in paid employment and grandparents look after their grandchildren.
- There are many more single-parent families as more couples divorce.
- More children are being brought up by cohabiting parents.
- Society treats homosexual sex the same way as heterosexual sex.
- Two people of the same sex can now form a legal union by signing a registration document in a civil partnership, giving them the same rights and treatment as an opposite-sex married couple.

Reasons for the changes

Cohabitation and marriage

- Effective contraception made it safer to have sex before marriage.
- Fewer people went to church and so were not encouraged to keep sex until after marriage.
- The media and celebrities made cohabitation look respectable and so it became more popular.
- The media showed sexual relationships outside marriage as the norm so more people thought sex outside marriage was acceptable.

Divorce

- New laws made divorce much cheaper and easier for ordinary people.
- Increased equality for women means that women are no longer prepared to accept unequal treatment from men, and if their husbands treat them badly, they will divorce them.
- Most married women depended on the husband's wages, but now many women are financially independent and can support themselves after a divorce.
- There has been a great change in how long people are likely to be married. Most divorces occur after ten years of marriage, which was the average length of a marriage 100 years ago.

Family life

- The popularity of cohabitation means there are more families where the parents are not married.
- The increase in divorce has led to an increase in re-marriage and so there are now many more re-constituted families.
- More mothers are in paid employment and use retired grandparents or close relatives to look after their children.
- The increase in divorce and the acceptance of unmarried mothers means there are more single-parent families.

Homosexuality

- Changes in the laws have made it easier to be openly homosexual and made society more aware of homosexuality.
- Medical research has shown that homosexuality is natural, leading people to accept equal status and rights for homosexual couples.
- Media coverage of gay celebrities has led to a greater acceptance of all gay people.
- The work of gay rights organisations has led to a greater acceptance of equal rights for homosexuals.

Evaluation questions

As these questions will always ask you to refer to Christianity, advice is given in subsequent topics.

Topic 3.3.2 Christian attitudes to sex outside marriage

Key points

- All Christians believe adultery is wrong as it breaks one of the Ten Commandments.
- Most Christians believe that sex before marriage is wrong because the Church and the Bible teach this.

Main points

Most Christians believe sex outside marriage is wrong because:

- God gave sex for the procreation of children who should be brought up in a Christian family, so sex should only take place within marriage.
- The Bible says that sex outside marriage is sinful and Christians should follow the teachings of the Bible.
- The Catechism says that pre-marital sex is wrong and Catholics should follow the teachings of the Catechism.
- All Christians are against adultery because it breaks the wedding vows.
- Adultery is also banned by the Ten Commandments, which all Christians should follow.
- Adultery is condemned by Jesus and all Christians should follow the teachings of Jesus.

Some Christians accept that couples may live together before marriage, but only in a long-term relationship leading to marriage.

Evaluation questions

You could be asked to argue for and against allowing sex before marriage.

1. People who agree with sex before marriage are likely to use such reasons as:
   - Sex is a natural result of two people being in love, and there is no reason for them waiting until they are married.
   - Modern contraception means that a couple can have sex without the risk of pregnancy, so unwanted children are not likely to result from sex before marriage.
   - Sex before marriage is now accepted by society and very few people think it is wrong.
2. Most Christians disagree with sex before marriage and so would use the reasons in the main points above.

You may also be asked to argue for and against getting married rather than living together.

1. Christians believe marriage is better than living together because:
   - Marriage is God's gift (a sacrament for Catholics), the way God says humans should have sex and bring up a family.
   - The Bible teaches that sex should only take place in marriage and that marriage is necessary for the upbringing of a Christian family.
   - The Church teaches that marriage is the basis of society and that living together without marriage is wrong.
   - Statistics show that married couples are more likely to stay together than cohabiting couples and that the children of married couples have a more stable and happy life.
2. People who believe living together is as good as marriage give such reasons as:
   - Couples who live together can be just as happy and committed as those who marry.
   - You cannot promise to stay with someone until death if you do not know what it will be like to live with them.
   - Living together brings all the commitment and joy of marriage without the legal complications.
   - Weddings are expensive and living together allows a couple to spend that money on the home, children, etc.

Topic 3.3.3 The purposes of marriage in Catholic Christianity

Main points

The Catholic Church teaches that marriage was created by God as a sacrament to unite a man and a woman so that:

- a couple can have a life-long relationship of love and faithfulness
- a couple can have the support and comfort of each other
- they can have the gift of children
- they can bring up a Christian family
- they can receive God's grace and strength through the sacrament.

How the purposes of marriage are shown in the wedding ceremony

The life-long relationship of love and faithfulness is shown in:

- the exchange of vows where the couple promise to be faithful to each other until death
- the Bible readings and homily on the nature of Christian marriage as a life-long relationship of love and faithfulness.

The couple having the support and comfort of each other is shown in:

- a preparation course before the wedding ceremony takes place which helps the couple to understand the nature of Catholic marriage and how to provide support and comfort for each other
- the priest asking the couple before the marriage vows if they will love and support each other.

The procreation of children is shown in:

- the priest asking the couple if they will accept children from God lovingly
- the readings, homily and prayers all refer to the acceptance of children as a key part of Catholic marriage.

The bringing up of a Christian family is shown in:

- the preparation course, which involves discussion about how the couple should bring up their children (baptism, First Confession and Communion, Catholic schooling, etc.)
- the priest asking the couple if they will accept children and bring them up according to the law of Christ and his Church.

Key points

Catholic marriage is for a life-long relationship of love and faithfulness and bringing up a Catholic family. These purposes can be seen in the marriage ceremony where the exchange of vows and rings, Bible readings, homily and prayers all emphasise them.

Evaluation questions

You may be asked to argue for and against a Catholic wedding service making a marriage last and/or be more successful.

1. To argue for a Catholic wedding service improving a marriage, you should use how the life-long relationship of love and faithfulness and how the couple have the support and comfort of each other are shown in the wedding service, as described in the main points on the left.

2. People who disagree are likely to use such arguments as:
   - Statistics show that couples who have a Catholic wedding are just as likely to divorce as those who marry in a registry office.
   - How much a couple love each other is more important than what type of wedding ceremony they have.
   - Couples are not likely to think about their wedding service when they are having a major row.

Topic 3.3.4 Christian attitudes to divorce

Main points

1 The Catholic attitude

The Catholic Church does not allow religious divorce or re-marriage. The only way a marriage between baptised Catholics can be ended is by the death of one of the partners.

However, the Catholic Church does allow civil divorce if that will be better for the children, but the couple are still married in the eyes of God and so cannot re-marry. Catholics have this attitude because:

- Jesus taught that divorce is wrong and Christians should follow his teachings.
- The couple have made a covenant with God which 'cannot be broken by any earthly power'.
- The Catechism teaches that a marriage cannot be dissolved and so religious divorce is impossible.
- There can be no re-marriage as there can be no religious divorce, and it would be both bigamy (having two husbands or wives) and adultery.

However, if it can be proved that the marriage was never a true Christian marriage, Catholics can have an annulment which makes them free to re-marry.

2 The attitude of non-Catholic Christians

Most non-Catholic Churches think that divorce is wrong, but allow it if the marriage has broken down and permit divorced people to remarry. These people are sometimes asked to promise that this time their marriage will be for life.

Non-Catholic Churches allow divorce because:

- Jesus allowed divorce in Matthew 19:9 for a partner's adultery.
- If a marriage has really broken down then the effects of the couple not divorcing would be a greater evil than the evil of divorce itself.
- If Christians repent and confess their sins they can be forgiven. This means a couple should have another chance at marriage if they are keen to make it work this time.
- These Churches believe it is better to divorce than to live in hatred and quarrel all the time.

Topic 3.3.5 Why family life is important for Catholics

Main points

Family life is important for Catholics because:

- One of the main purposes of Catholic marriage is to have children and bring them up in a Catholic environment so that they become good Catholics.
- Catholicism teaches that the family was created by God as the basis of society and the only place for the upbringing of children.
- Catholic teaching on divorce shows that the family is too important to be broken up by divorce.
- Without the family, children would not learn the difference between right and wrong.
- The family is the place where children learn about the faith through baptism, First Communion, etc. So the family is very important for the faith to continue and grow as it is the family that brings children into the faith.

However, the Church (from Jesus) teaches that the Christian family is the most important family which is why Catholic priests, nuns and monks leave their families so that they can serve God.

Key points

Catholics believe that the family is important because:

- it is taught in the Bible and Catechism
- Catholic marriage services refer to bringing up a family as one of the main purposes of marriage
- Catholics believe that the family was created by God.

Evaluation questions

You may be asked to argue for and against family life being more important for religious than non-religious people.

1. To argue for family life being more important for religious than non-religious people, you can use any of the main points above for family life being important for Catholics. You could also use points from Topics 3.3.6 and 3.3.7 (pages 42 and 43).

2. Arguments against family life being more important for religious than non-religious people:
   - Many non-religious people see their family as being the most important thing in their lives whereas many religious people see their religion as more important than their family.
   - Most non-religious people have just as good a family life as religious people.
   - Non-religious families can respect their children more because they do not have to force them to try to be religious.
   - Religion cannot make a difference to how much parents love their children, and children love their parents.

Topic 3.3.6 How Catholic parishes help with the upbringing of children

Catholic parishes help parents with the upbringing of their children by:

- supporting the local Catholic schools
- running classes for First Communion and Confirmation
- running children's liturgies
- running youth clubs and youth activities.

Main points

- Most parishes have a local Catholic primary and secondary school connected to them. This Catholic education helps parents because it teaches children right from wrong and helps parents to fulfil their marriage and baptism promises to bring their children up as Catholics.
- Parishes run classes to prepare children for First Confession, Communion and Confirmation, helping parents with the Catholic upbringing of their children.
- Some parishes run children's liturgies which help parents to bring their children up as good Catholics and give parents and their children the spiritual strength of the Mass.
- Some parishes also run youth clubs and youth activities so that children are kept off the streets and away from bad influences.

Evaluation questions

You may be asked to argue for and against Catholic parishes not doing enough to help with the upbringing of children.

1. To argue for, you should use points in the main points above.

2. People who disagree are likely to use reasons such as:
   - not all parishes have children's liturgies
   - not all parishes run youth activities
   - some parishes make children and young people feel unwanted because they are thought to disturb the seriousness of worship.

Topic 3.3.7 How Catholic parishes help to keep families together

Main points

Because family life is so important, Catholic parishes offer lots of help to keep families together:

- During Mass the priest may remind parents of their marriage vows and other reasons not to divorce.
- The parish priest has a duty to give help and advice to couples having family problems.
- The Church has a national programme of support for marriage and family life (*Celebrating Family: Blessed, Broken, Living Love*), and provides support to parishes to keep families together through the Marriage and Family Life Project Office.
- The Church has provided resources for parishes to be more family friendly so that family life can be strengthened by families celebrating Mass together.
- The Church has produced a series of leaflets to help parishes understand and meet the needs of families facing challenges such as divorce and re-marriage, bereavement, disability and gay or lesbian family members.
- Many parishes also provide financial support for families in need and have links to national Catholic charities such as Catholic Marriage Care.

Key points

Catholic parishes help to keep families together by:

- welcoming families to worship together
- the priest offering help and advice for family problems
- homilies at Mass encouraging and strengthening family values
- providing leaflets on how to deal with family problems
- providing financial support and links to Catholic family charities.

Evaluation questions

You may be asked to argue for and against the idea that Catholic parishes help to keep families together.

1. To argue for, you should use the main points above.
2. People who disagree are likely to use such arguments as:
   - Statistics show that Catholic families are just as likely to break up as other families.

- Not all parishes provide the support outlined above.
- Some parishes would not provide support for families who had lapsed from the faith or who were having problems over issues such as needing infertility treatments which are banned by the Church.

Topic 3.3.8 Christian attitudes to homosexuality

Main points

There are several attitudes to homosexuality in Christianity. The main ones are:

1 The Catholic attitude

The Catholic attitude is that being a homosexual is not a sin but that homosexual sexual activity is a sin. The Catholic Church asks homosexuals to live without any sexual activity and believes they will be helped to do this by the sacraments of the Church. The Church believes that it is sinful to criticise homosexuals or attack their behaviour. Catholics have this attitude because:

- The Bible condemns homosexual sexual activity.
- It is the tradition of the Church that any sexual activity should have the possibility of creating children.
- It is the teaching of the Magisterium which Catholics should believe.
- The Church teaches that people cannot help their sexual orientation, but they can control their sexual activity.
- Discriminating against people because of their sexual orientation is similar to racism, which is sinful.

2 The Evangelical Protestant attitude

Many Evangelical Protestants believe that homosexuality is a sin and that homosexuals can be changed by the power of the Holy Spirit. The reasons for this attitude are:

- The Bible says that homosexuality is a sin and they believe that the Bible is the direct word of God.
- They believe that the salvation of Christ can remove all sins, including homosexuality.
- All the Churches have taught that homosexuality is wrong, even though some now say it is not.

However, the Evangelical Alliance has recently condemned homophobia and said churches should welcome homosexuals.

3 The Liberal Protestant attitude

Many Liberal Protestants welcome homosexuals into the Church, and accept homosexual relationships. Some Liberal Protestants provide blessings for civil partnerships. The reasons for this attitude are:

- They believe that the Bible texts condemning homosexuality show beliefs at the time rather than being the word of God.
- They feel that the major Christian belief in love and acceptance means that homosexuals must be accepted.
- Many believe that if homosexual Christians feel the Holy Spirit approves of their homosexuality, it must be true.
- They believe that Christians should be open and honest and so gay Christians should not be made to tell lies and pretend to be heterosexual.

Evaluation questions

You may be asked to argue for and against giving equal rights to homosexuals (similar arguments could be used for questions on whether Christians or religious people can be homosexual).

1. Arguments for giving equal rights:
   - British law gives equal rights to homosexuals, and equal rights are part of their basic human rights.
   - Medical research has shown that homosexuality is probably genetic and therefore natural, so homosexuals should have equal status and rights.
   - Many liberal Christians feel that the major Christian belief in love and acceptance means that homosexuals must be given equal rights.

2. Arguments against giving equal rights to homosexuals:
   - The Bible condemns homosexual sexual activity, so homosexuals cannot have equal rights.
   - It is the tradition of the Church that any sexual activity should have the possibility of creating children, therefore homosexuals should not be allowed to be sexually active.
   - The Churches have always taught that homosexuality is wrong and so homosexuals should not be given equal rights.

You may also be asked to argue for and against civil partnerships.

1. Arguments for civil partnerships:
   - They allow homosexual couples to commit themselves to each other and encourage stable sexual relationships.
   - They allow homosexual couples to share their belongings, pensions, etc. in just the same way as heterosexual couples.
   - They are a way of encouraging the Christian virtues of love and faithfulness among homosexuals.

2. Arguments against civil partnerships:
   - Christianity teaches that God gave marriage for a man and a woman, not two people of the same sex.
   - One of the purposes of Christian marriage is for the procreation of children and as homosexuals cannot procreate, they should not marry.
   - Christians who believe homosexuals should not be sexually active cannot accept civil partnerships because they encourage homosexual sexual activity.

Topic 3.3.9 Different methods of contraception

Evaluation questions

Any evaluation questions are likely to ask you to refer to Christianity, so the advice is given after the next topic (Topic 3.3.10, page 47).

Main points

Contraception allows couples to control the number of children by allowing sex without pregnancy. It is now estimated that 90 per cent of the sexually active population of childbearing age in the UK use some form of contraception.

There are two very different types of contraception.

1 Natural methods of contraception

The most used natural method is known as natural family planning (NFP). It reduces the chance of becoming pregnant by planning sex around the times in the month when a woman is at her most infertile. It works best if taught by an experienced NFP teacher.

Another method measures hormone levels in the urine. If used properly, these methods can be 94 per cent effective.

To be used properly, natural methods require a couple to be in a loving, stable relationship (as sexually active Catholics should be). They do not involve any drugs or any risk of an early abortion. Although they do not prevent sexually transmitted diseases, this should not affect a married Catholic couple who are faithful.

2 Artificial methods of contraception

There are several types of artificial contraception: condoms prevent the sperm from reaching the egg; the pill stops a woman from producing eggs; the coil and the morning-after pill bring about an early abortion if the egg fertilises.

Artificial methods can be used in any form of sexual relationship, however casual. Condoms are also effective in preventing the transmission of sexually transmitted diseases (especially AIDS).

Topic 3.3.10 Different Christian attitudes to contraception

Main points

1 The Catholic attitude

The Catholic Church says couples should limit family size through using natural family planning rather than artificial methods of contraception because:

- Pope Pius XI condemned all forms of artificial contraception.
- Pope Pius XII declared that Catholics could use natural methods of contraception.
- Pope Paul VI stated that the only allowable forms of contraception are natural methods, and this teaching has been confirmed in the Catechism of the Catholic Church.
- The Church teaches that all sex should be unitive (bringing the couple together) and creative (bringing new life).
- Some artificial contraceptives bring about a very early abortion (abortifacient).

2 The attitude of non-Catholic Christians

Almost all non-Catholic Christians believe that all forms of contraception are permissible because:

- Christianity is about love and justice, and contraception improves women's health and raises the standard of living.
- God created sex for enjoyment and to strengthen marriage so there does not have to be the possibility of creation of children.
- There is nothing in the Bible that forbids the use of contraception.
- All the non-Catholic Churches say Christians can use contraception to limit family size.
- They believe that using condoms is the best way to combat HIV/AIDS.

> ## Key points
>
> - The Catholic Church teaches that using artificial methods of contraception to stop a baby being conceived is wrong. God gave humans sex in order to create children. Natural methods of contraception are acceptable.
> - Other Christians allow the use of contraception because they believe God gave humans sex to strengthen a married relationship.

Evaluation questions

You may be asked to argue for and against Christians being allowed to use artificial methods of contraception.

1. To argue for artificial methods contraception use the non-Catholic reasons for allowing contraception in the second main point above.

2. To argue against artificial methods of contraception use the Catholic reasons for not allowing contraception in the first main point above.

Topic 3.3.11 How an issue from marriage and the family has been presented in one form of the media

Key points

When studying the presentation of an issue from marriage and the family in the media, you must be able to explain:

- why the issue was chosen
- how it was presented
- whether the presentation treated religious beliefs fairly
- whether the presentation treated religious people fairly.

Main points

You have to study how *one* issue from marriage and the family has been presented in *one* form of the media.

From your class notes you should have:

- Notes on why the issue is important and why you think the producers decided to focus on this issue.
- An outline of how the issue was presented, listing the main events and the way the events explored the issue.
- Notes on the way religious beliefs are treated in the presentation of the issue.
- Four pieces of evidence on whether you think the presentation was fair to religious beliefs.
- Four pieces of evidence on whether you think the presentation was fair to religious people.

Evaluation questions

Although you are unlikely to be asked an evaluation question on this topic, if you were, it would be about whether the media treat religious beliefs or people fairly.

1. To argue that media are fair, you should use:
   - The evidence you have from one form of the media for the religious beliefs being treated fairly.
   - The evidence you have from one form of the media for religious people being treated fairly.

2. To argue that media are not fair, you should use:
   - The evidence you have from one form of the media for the religious beliefs not being treated fairly.
   - The evidence you have from one form of the media for religious people not being treated fairly.

How to answer questions on Section 3.3

You should already know the basics about how to answer questions from Section 3.1, pages 15–17, but here is an answer to a whole question on Section 3.3 with a commentary to help you.

Question a)
What is promiscuity?   (2 marks)

Answer

Sleeping around.

    One mark for a partially correct answer.

Answer

Having sex with a number of partners without commitment.

    Two marks for a correct definition.

Question b)
Do you think sex outside marriage is wrong?
Give TWO reasons for your point of view. (4 marks)

Answer

Yes, because adultery is cheating on your marriage partner ...

    One mark for a reason.

... and breaking your wedding vows.

    Two marks because the reason is developed.

Also, it is breaking the commandments ...

    Three marks because a second reason is given.

... because the sixth commandment says 'You shall not commit adultery'.

    Four marks because the second reason is developed.

    Total = four marks.

Question c)
Explain why some Christian Churches allow divorce and some do not.   (8 marks)

Answer

The Catholic Church does not allow divorce because Jesus taught that divorce is wrong and Christians should follow his teachings.

    LEVEL 1: two marks for a reason for one attitude expressed in basic English.

Also, the Catechism teaches that a marriage cannot be dissolved and so religious divorce is impossible because the couple have made a covenant with God which 'cannot be broken by any earthly power'.

    LEVEL 2: by giving a second reason for the attitude, the answer goes up to level 2 and because the answer is written in clear English it would gain four marks.

Non-Catholic Churches allow divorce because Jesus allowed divorce in Matthew 19:9 for a partner's adultery.

    LEVEL 3: by adding another attitude with a reason the answer moves up to level 3 and because the answer is written in a clear style of English with some use of specialist vocabulary (Catholic, Jesus, Catechism, covenant, earthly power, non-Catholic, Matthew, adultery) it would gain six marks.

They believe that if a marriage has really broken down then the effects of the couple not divorcing would be a greater evil than the evil of divorce itself. These Churches believe it is better to divorce than live in hatred and quarrel all the time.

    LEVEL 4: by adding a further reason for the second attitude, the answer moves up to level 4 and because it is written in a clear and correct style of English with extra specialist vocabulary (broken down, greater evil, Churches) it would gain eight marks – full marks.

Section 3.4 **Religion and community cohesion**

KEY WORDS FOR SECTION 3.4

Community cohesion	a common vision and shared sense of belonging for all groups in society
Discrimination	treating people less favourably because of their ethnicity/gender/colour/sexuality/age/class
Ethnic minority	a member of an ethnic group (race) which is much smaller than the majority group
Interfaith marriages	marriage where the husband and wife are from different religions
Multi-ethnic society	many different races and cultures living together in one society
Multi-faith society	many different religions living together in one society
Prejudice	believing some people are inferior or superior without even knowing them
Racial harmony	different races/colours living together happily
Racism	the belief that some races are superior to others
Religious freedom	the right to practise your religion and change your religion
Religious pluralism	accepting all religions as having an equal right to coexist
Sexism	discriminating against people because of their gender (being male or female)

Topic 3.4.1 How and why attitudes to the roles of men and women have changed in the United Kingdom

Main points

During the second half of the nineteenth century it became the accepted view that married women should stay at home and look after the children. However, between 1882 and 1975 women gained the rights to:

- keep their property separate from that of their husband
- vote in elections and become councillors and MPs
- receive the same pay as men for the same work.

In 1975, the Sex Discrimination Act aimed to reduce sexism in society by making it illegal to discriminate in employment on grounds of gender or whether someone is married.

Attitudes to the roles of men and women have been slower to change and women are still more likely to do all the housework and have fewer promotion prospects and lower salaries than men.

Why attitudes have changed

- The work of the suffragette movement showed that women were no longer prepared to be treated as second class citizens.
- During the First and Second World Wars, women had to take on many of the jobs previously done by men and did these jobs just as well as men.
- The development of equal rights for women in other countries made it difficult to claim they were not needed in the UK.
- Social and industrial developments in the 1950s and 1960s led to the need for more women workers.
- The UN Declaration of Human Rights and the development of the feminist movement meant equal rights had to be accepted.
- The Labour governments of 1964–70 and 1974–9 were dedicated to equal rights for women.

Key points

Attitudes to the roles of men and women have changed greatly:

- women now have equal rights
- men and women are expected to share roles in the home.

Attitudes have changed because of:

- the feminist movement
- social and industrial changes
- the effects of the world wars.

Evaluation questions

Any questions are likely to ask you to refer to Christianity so the advice on evaluation questions comes with Topic 3.4.2, page 54.

Topic 3.4.2 Different Christian attitudes to equal rights for women in religion

Evaluation questions

1. For arguments for women having equal rights in religion, use the reasons for the modern Protestant attitude in point 3 and the first two bullets listing the reasons for the Catholic attitude in point 1.

2. For arguments against, use the reasons for the traditional Protestant attitude in point 2 and the last two bullets listing the reasons for the Catholic attitude in point 1.

Main points

There are different attitudes to equal rights for women in religion in Christianity.

1 The Catholic attitude

The Catholic Church teaches that men and women should have equal rights in society and in religion except that they cannot be part of the ordained ministry (deacons, priests and bishops). They have this attitude because:

- The creation story in Genesis 1 says that God created male and female at the same time in his image and therefore of equal status.
- It is the teaching of the Catholic Catechism that men and women are equal, and should have equal rights in life and society.
- Only men can be priests because the apostles were all men, and priests and bishops are successors of the apostles.
- Only men can be priests because Jesus was a man and the priest represents Jesus in the Mass.

2 The traditional attitude of Protestant Christianity

Many Evangelical Protestants teach that men and women have separate and different roles and so cannot have equal rights in religion. Women should not speak in church and only men can be Church leaders and teachers.

They have this attitude because:

- In the Bible, St Paul teaches that women should not teach or speak in church.
- St Paul also uses the story of Adam and Eve in Genesis to show that men have been given more rights by God because Adam was created first.
- Although Jesus had women followers, he chose only men as his twelve apostles.
- It has always been the tradition of the Church that only men should be leaders.

3 The modern attitude of Protestant Christianity

Many Protestant Churches (e.g. Church of England, Methodist, United Reformed Church, Baptist) give men and women equal rights, and have women ministers and priests, because:

- The creation story in Genesis 1 says that God created male and female at the same time in his image and therefore of equal status.
- In some of his letters, Paul teaches that men and women are equal in Christ.
- There is evidence from the Gospels that Jesus treated women as his equals, for example:
  - he had women disciples who stayed with him at the cross unlike the male disciples who ran away
  - after his resurrection, Jesus appeared first to his women disciples.
- There is some evidence that there were women priests in the early Church.

Topic 3.4.3 The nature of the United Kingdom as a multi-ethnic society

Main points

The UK has always been a **multi-ethnic society**. In the 2001 Census, only 7.9 per cent of the UK's population came from **ethnic minorities** (although this percentage changes greatly in different areas).

1 The problems of discrimination and racism

- Racially prejudiced employers will not give jobs to certain ethnic groups; religiously prejudiced employers will not give jobs to certain religious groups.
- Prejudiced landlords are likely to refuse accommodation to certain ethnic groups or religions.
- If teachers are prejudiced against certain ethnic minorities or religious groups, they will discriminate against them in their teaching so that those pupils might not achieve the results they should.
- Prejudiced police officers will discriminate against certain ethnic or religious groups, for example by stopping and searching them when they have no real reason for so doing.

The effects of these problems:

- If certain groups feel that they are being treated unfairly by society then they will begin to work against that society.
- Some politicians believe that young black people turn to crime because they feel they will not be able to get good well-paid jobs because of **discrimination**.
- Some politicians believe that young Muslims have been turning to extremist Islamic groups because they feel they have no chance of success in a prejudiced British society.
- **Racism** and discrimination can lead to groups like the BNP (British National Party) stirring up hatred and violence.

2 The benefits of living in a multi-ethnic society

- People of different ethnic groups and nationalities will get to know and like each other, and probably intermarry.
- More progress will be made in a multi-ethnic society because new people will bring in new ideas and new ways of doing things.
- Life is more interesting with a much greater variety of food, music, fashion and entertainment.
- A multi-ethnic society helps people to live and work in a world of multi-national companies and economic interdependence between all nations.

Key points

- Britain has many ethnic minorities and so is a multi-ethnic society.
- Multi-ethnic societies have many benefits, such as advancing more quickly because they have a greater variety of ideas.
- A multi-ethnic society needs equal opportunities and treatment to work, so prejudice and discrimination cause major problems in such a society because they do not treat everyone equally.

Evaluation questions

You may be asked to argue for and against living in a multi-ethnic society.

1. For arguments for multi-ethnic societies use point 2 opposite.

2. People who argue against multi-ethnic societies use such arguments as:
   - Different ethnic groups living in one society are likely to come into conflict with each other if they disagree with each other.
   - Multi-ethnic societies can lead to the loss of the culture of the original group (e.g. the effect of non-Cornish ethnic groups living in Cornwall has led to the disappearance of the Cornish language).
   - If every ethnic group had its own country, there would be no conflict.

Topic 3.4.4 Government action to promote community cohesion in the United Kingdom

Main points

A multi-ethnic society needs to promote community cohesion in order to remove the problems of prejudice, discrimination and racism. The British government promotes community cohesion by:

- Passing the Race Relations Act which makes it unlawful to discriminate against anyone because of race, colour, nationality, ethnic or national origins; or to stir up racial hatred.
- Passing the Crime and Disorder Act which allows more severe punishment for offences which involve racial or religious hatred.
- Passing the Racial and Religious Hatred Act which makes it an offence to use threatening words or behaviour about religious beliefs or lack of belief.
- Establishing the Equality and Human Rights Commission which promotes equality and human rights for all, and works to get rid of discrimination and to build good relations.
- Making community cohesion part of the National Curriculum in schools.

Why community cohesion is important for multi-ethnic and multi-faith societies

- Without community cohesion different groups have different ideas about what society should be like and this can lead to violence. For example, a lack of community cohesion in Oldham, Burnley and Bradford led to racially/religiously motivated street rioting in 2001.
- The 7 July 2005 London bombers were British citizens who had lost their sense of allegiance to Britain.
- In countries without community cohesion (such as Iraq, Kosovo, Kashmir) violence becomes a way of life.
- Lack of community cohesion makes it impossible for people to co-operate in the way modern civilised living needs.

Community cohesion is therefore about:

- how to avoid the bad effects of prejudice and discrimination
- how to encourage different groups to work together
- how to ensure respect for others while building up loyal citizens of the same society.

Evaluation questions

You may be asked to argue for and against the need for/importance of government action to promote community cohesion.

1. For arguments for the importance of/need for government action use the reasons listed under 'Why community cohesion is important for multi-ethnic and multi-faith societies' opposite.

2. Those who argue against government action to promote community cohesion are likely to use such arguments as:
   - If people are forced to co-operate, it might lead to fighting and hatred of different groups.
   - The UK has always believed in multi-culturalism – allowing people from different ethnic and cultural backgrounds to live in the UK while following their own culture – which avoids conflict.
   - It does not matter if different cultural communities follow their own ideas about society as long as they all obey British laws.
   - Community cohesion is not possible, the rich have different ideas from the poor, the workers from the employers, etc.

Topic 3.4.5 Why Catholics should help to promote racial harmony

Main points

Catholics should try to promote (bring about) racial harmony because:

- In the Parable of the Good Samaritan, Jesus showed that races who hated each other (as did the Jews and Samaritans) should love each other as neighbours.
- St Peter had a vision from God telling him not to discriminate because God has no favourites among the races.
- St Paul taught that all races are equal in Christ since God created all races in his image.
- The Catholic Church has members from every race. Over 30 per cent of the world is Christian and 70 per cent of Christians are non-white, non-European.
- There are Catholic cardinals and bishops of every race and colour of skin.
- The Catholic Church is dedicated to fighting racism in all its forms as seen in the teachings of the Catechism and encyclicals from Pope John Paul II and Benedict XVI.

Evaluation questions

You could be asked to argue for and against religion/Christianity being the best way to bring about racial harmony.

1. For reasons for, use the main points above.
2. Arguments against could include:
   - Some Christian groups work against racial harmony, for example the Ku Klux Klan.
- Politics is a better way of bringing about racial harmony, for example the USA now has a black President, but the Catholic Church does not have a black Pope.
- Not everyone is religious and so laws which give everyone equal rights are more likely to bring about racial harmony.

Topic 3.4.6 The work of the Catholic Church to help asylum seekers and immigrant workers

Main points

1 How the Catholic Church helps asylum seekers and immigrant workers

- The Catholic Church in England and Wales has set up the Office for Refugee Policy (ORP) which keeps a watch on what is happening and prepares reports on immigration issues for the bishops. It also represents the bishops on immigration issues nationally and internationally and helps ordinary Catholics to work with refugees.
- In April 2008, the Catholic Bishops' Conference put forward a range of ways in which local parishes can help immigrants. These include: making important leaflets available in immigrant languages, providing English-language classes, collecting equipment to help migrants to set up home.
- Parishes with a lot of immigrants have set up legal advice clinics to help immigrants cope with the legal issues of settling in the UK.
- Some parishes provide Masses in other languages so that immigrant workers can maintain their faith and worship.

2 Why the Catholic Church helps asylum seekers and migrant workers

- The Bible teaches that God is a God of justice who requires his followers to behave justly and seek justice for everyone.
- The Catholic Church teaches that no one should be oppressed and that Christians should seek justice for the oppressed.
- It is the teaching of Jesus in the Parable of the Good Samaritan and the Parable of the Sheep and Goats.
- Jesus himself was a refugee and asylum seeker when the holy family fled to Egypt to avoid Herod's slaughter of the innocents.

> ## Key points
>
> The Catholic Church helps refugees and immigrant workers though a special office which tells parishes how they can help and which deals with publicity. Parishes offer help with things like legal problems and English-language classes.
>
> The Church helps because of the teachings of Jesus such as the parables of the Good Samaritan and the Sheep and Goats.

Evaluation questions

You may be asked to argue for and against the Catholic Church helping asylum seekers and immigrant workers.

1. To argue for, you should use the reasons why the Catholic Church helps, from part 2 above.

2. People who argue against use such reasons as:
   - The more help Catholics give, the more asylum seekers and immigrant workers will arrive in the UK which is already full.
   - It is better to give people help in their own countries through CAFOD.

- The Church should be focusing on stopping the wars that force people to become asylum seekers.

You may be asked to argue for and against the idea that the Church is not doing enough to help asylum seekers and immigrant workers.

1. To argue for, you should use such reasons as:
   - not all parishes are providing help
   - not all parishes take notice of what the ORP says
   - some Catholics in some parishes are still racist.

2. To argue against you should use the points from part 1 above.

Topic 3.4.7 The United Kingdom as a multi-faith society

Key points

Britain is a multi-faith society because several religions are practised here and everyone is free to practise their own religion. A multi-faith society has many benefits such as religious freedom and the opportunity to find out about, and think more deeply about, different religions.

Main points

Many societies were mono-faith (having only one religion) until the twentieth century, but Britain has had believers in different faiths for many years and by the end of the twentieth century Muslims, Jews, Hindus, Sikhs, Buddhists and other religions were settled in the UK, so that it is a truly multi-faith society.

The benefits of living in a multi-faith society

- People can learn about other religions and this can help them to see what religions have in common.
- People from different religions may practise their religion more seriously and this may make people think about how they practise their own religion.
- People may come to understand why different religions believe what they do and this may make people think more seriously about their own beliefs.
- People are likely to become a lot more understanding about and respectful of each other's religions.
- Religious freedom and understanding will exist in a multi-faith society and this may help to stop religious conflicts.
- A multi-faith society may even make some people think more about religion as they come across religious ideas they have never thought about before.

Evaluation questions

You could be asked to argue for and against living in a multi-faith society.

1. To argue for living in a multi-faith society, use the reasons listed under 'The benefits of living in a multi-faith society' above.

2. People who are firm believers in one religion might be against multi-faith societies because:
   - They encourage children to look at other religions, and children might desert their parents' religion.

- Children from different religions may want to marry each other, and interfaith marriages can create problems for religious parents.
- They can make it difficult to follow a particular religion because society cannot be organised for every religion's different rules.
- They can make it difficult for believers to spread their faith because people from other religions might object to them saying that their religion is the best one.

Topic 3.4.8 Differences among Christians in their attitudes to other religions

Main points

All Christians believe that everyone should have the right to follow whatever religion they want (religious freedom), but:

1 Catholics and many other Christians believe that people can come to God through different religions, but only Christianity has the full truth (inclusivism). They have this attitude because:
   - It is the teaching of the Church in the Catechism.
   - They believe Jesus is the Son of God who shows what God is like.
   - The Bible teaches that Christianity has the full truth and that salvation (going to heaven) comes through believing in Jesus, though God can be contacted by other religions.

2 Some Evangelical Protestant Christians believe Christianity is the only way to come to God and so they should try to convert everyone to Christianity (exclusivism) because:
   - Jesus said that he was the only way to God.
   - They think converting their non-Christian neighbour is the way to love them because it is the only way of getting them into heaven.
   - Jesus said Christians have to convert all the nations.

3 Some Liberal Protestant Christians believe that all religions are equal and are just different ways of finding God (pluralism). They have this attitude because:
   - They do not regard the Bible as the word of God.
   - They believe that God is a force like gravity which can be discovered by humans in different ways.
   - They see Muslims, Hindus, Sikhs, etc. living good holy lives.
   - They believe there is room for other religions in heaven because Jesus said there are many rooms in heaven.

Key points

All Christians believe in religious freedom, but:
- some Christians believe there is some truth in other religions
- some Christians believe Christianity is the only true religion
- some Christians believe all religions are a path to God.

Evaluation questions

You could be asked to argue for and against Christianity being the only true religion/only Christians being able to go to heaven.

1. To argue for, you should use the reasons for the Evangelical Protestant view in point 2 above.

2. To argue against, you should use the reasons for the Catholic and Liberal Protestant views in points 1 and 3 above.

Topic 3.4.9 Issues raised for religion by a multi-faith society

Main points

For a multi-faith society to work, people need to have the same rights regardless of the religion they do or do not belong to (religious pluralism). A multi-faith society cannot accept any one religion as being the true one, and the people living in the society must be free to choose or reject any or all of the religions practised in the society. This can raise a number of issues for religion.

Conversion

1 Many religions see it as their duty to convert everyone because:
   - They believe that their religion is the only true religion.
   - They believe that the only way for the followers of other religions to get to heaven is for them to be converted.
   - Their holy books teach them that they should convert non-believers.

2 Trying to convert other religions can cause major problems because:
   - Treating people differently because of their religion and trying to convert other religions is discriminating against those who do not have the same faith as you.
   - It is impossible to say all other religions are wrong unless you have studied all of them and no one who is trying to convert others has done this.
   - Trying to convert others can lead to arguments and even violence when people are told their religion is wrong.

Bringing up children

A multi-faith society requires everyone (including children) to have religious freedom and be able to choose which religion to follow, or to reject religion. It also requires that children should learn about the different religions in the society. This causes problems for many religious believers because:

- Most religions encourage parents to ensure that their children are brought up in their religion and become members of it.
- Most religions teach that only those who follow their religion will have a good life after death, and parents worry what will happen to their children after death if they do not stay in their religion.
- Social and peer pressures compel parents to exert pressure on their children to remain in the faith.
- Children educated in state schools are tempted away from religious lifestyles into the lifestyles of other non-religious teenagers.

Interfaith marriages

In a multi-faith society, young people of different faiths are going to meet, fall in love and want to marry. This can raise problems because:

- Often both couples must be members of the same religion to have a religious wedding ceremony.
- There is a question of which religion the children of the marriage will be brought up in.
- There is also the problem of what will happen to the couple after death. If the husband is Christian and the wife Hindu, will the husband go to heaven and the wife be reborn?
- The parents and relatives of the couple often feel that they have been betrayed.

Unless these issues are dealt with, then religion itself can be working against community cohesion and promoting conflict and hatred.

Evaluation questions

You may be asked to argue for and against having the right to convert others.

1. For arguments for having the right, use the reasons listed in point 1 opposite under 'Conversion'.

2. For arguments against, use the reasons listed in point 2 opposite under 'Conversion'.

You may be asked to argue for and against having the right to bring up children in one faith only.

1. For arguments in favour of the right, use the reasons listed under 'Bringing up children' opposite.

2. The main arguments against children being brought up in one faith only include:
   - It is a human right to have freedom of religion and so children need to learn about more than one religion before they choose which to follow, or not follow.
   - A multi-faith society needs its members to respect all religions and children need to learn about other religions if they are to respect the followers of that religion.
   - Children who are brought up knowing only one religion cannot really believe it because they have not compared it with anything else, so they cannot know that it is the best religion.

You may be asked to argue for and against interfaith marriages.

1. The main arguments for interfaith marriages are:
   - It is a human right to be able to marry anyone you want to (especially if you are in love with them).
   - Interfaith marriages will encourage community cohesion as families from different faiths become one family.
   - The children of interfaith marriages will have true religious freedom as they learn about both their parents' religions and can choose between them.

2. For arguments against interfaith marriages use the reasons listed under 'Interfaith marriages' above.

Topic 3.4.10 Ways in which religions work to promote community cohesion in the United Kingdom

Main points

The different religions in the UK are beginning to work to promote community cohesion in the following ways.

1 Different religions are beginning to work with other religions to try to discover what is the same in their religions (e.g. Judaism, Islam and Christianity believe in the prophets Abraham and Moses), and from this work out ways of living together without trying to convert each other.

2 Some religious groups are developing ways of helping interfaith marriages.
- Many Protestant Churches and Liberal or Reform Jewish synagogues have developed special wedding services for mixed faith couples.
- Some religious leaders have set up a website (www.interfaithmarriage.org.uk) to offer help and advice to couples from different religions.

3 The problem of bringing up children is being dealt with in different ways:
- Some Protestant Christian Churches and Liberal or Reform Jewish synagogues encourage mixed faith parents to bring up their children in both faiths.
- Leaders from the Church of England, Hindu, Sikh, Catholic, Muslim, Jewish and Buddhist faiths have agreed to teach the main religions practised in the UK in their schools.

4 The main way in which religions are trying to promote community cohesion is through working together in special groups:
- There are national groups such as the Inter Faith Network for the UK.
- There are also groups in most towns and cities bringing together the different religious groups in an area, for example the Glasgow Forum of Faiths.
- There are individual places of worship which work together.

Evaluation questions

You may be asked to argue for and against whether religions are doing enough to promote community cohesion in the UK.

1. You can use any of the points above to argue that they are doing enough to promote community cohesion.

2. The main arguments against are:
   - All religions have groups that are still teaching that all other religions are wrong.

- Most Christians, Muslims, etc. are unaware of what is going on with other faiths; it is only a few leaders who are involved in the work.
- Few religious believers look at the beliefs of other religions and try to work out which is true.
- Most religious groups are too busy looking after their own followers to try to make links with other faiths.

Topic 3.4.11 How an issue from religion and community cohesion has been dealt with in the media

Main points

You have to study how *one* issue from religion and community cohesion has been presented in *one* form of the media.

From your class notes you should have:

- Notes on why the issue is important and why you think the producers decided to focus on this issue.
- An outline of how the issue was presented, listing the main events and the way the events explored the issue.
- Notes on the way religious beliefs are treated in the presentation of the issue.
- Four pieces of evidence on whether you think the presentation was fair to religious beliefs.
- Four pieces of evidence on whether you think the presentation was fair to religious people.

Key points

When studying the presentation of an issue from religion and community cohesion in the media, you must be able to explain:

- why the issue was chosen
- how it was presented
- whether the presentation treated religious beliefs fairly
- whether the presentation treated religious people fairly.

Evaluation questions

Although you are unlikely to be asked an evaluation question on this topic, if you were, it would be about whether the media treat religious beliefs or people fairly.

1. To argue that media are fair, you should use:
   - The evidence you have from one form of the media for the religious beliefs being treated fairly.
   - The evidence you have from one form of the media for religious people being treated fairly.

2. To argue that media are not fair, you should use:
   - The evidence you have from one form of the media for the religious beliefs not being treated fairly.
   - The evidence you have from one form of the media for religious people not being treated fairly.

SECTION 3.4 TEST

SECTION 3.4: Religion and community cohesion

Answer both questions.

1. a) What is an ethnic minority? (2 marks)

   b) Do you think men and women should have equal roles in life?
   Give two reasons for your point of view. (4 marks)

   c) Explain why racism and discrimination bring problems to a
   multi-ethnic society. (8 marks)

   d) 'It is easy for different religions to work together in the UK.'

   (i) Do you agree? Give reasons for your opinion. (3 marks)

   (ii) Give reasons why some people may disagree with you. (3 marks)

   In your answer you should refer to Christianity.

   (Total: 20 marks)

2. a) What is interfaith marriage? (2 marks)

   b) Do you think Christians should work for racial harmony?
   Give two reasons for your point of view. (4 marks)

   c) Explain how the government is working to promote community
   cohesion in the UK. (8 marks)

   d) 'If everyone were religious, there would be no racism.'

   (i) Do you agree? Give reasons for your opinion. (3 marks)

   (ii) Give reasons why some people may disagree with you. (3 marks)

   In your answer you should refer to Christianity.

   (Total: 20 marks)

You should now use the mark scheme in Appendix 1, page 135, to mark your
answers, and the self-help tables in Appendix 1, pages 136–137, to see how you
can improve your performance. If you need more help with the mark scheme for
these questions, go to www.hoddereducation.co.uk/catholicchristianity

KEY WORDS FOR SECTION 10.1

Atonement	reconciliation between God and humanity
Catechism	official teaching of the Roman Catholic Church
Compassion	a feeling of pity which makes one want to help the sufferer
Creeds	statements of Christian beliefs
Faith	firm belief without logical proof
Incarnation	the belief that God took human form in Jesus
Monotheism	belief in one God
Repentance	the act of being sorry for wrongdoing and deciding not to do it again
Salvation	the act of delivering from sin, or saving from evil
Trinity	the belief that God is three in one
Unity	God's way of being one
Virgin Birth	the belief that Jesus was not conceived through sex

Topic 10.1.1 The meaning, and importance for Christians, of believing in God as Unity and Trinity

Key points

- Christians believe in the Unity of God and also that God is a Trinity. God's Unity helps them understand the power and importance of God because there is only one God and Christians should worship him. God's Trinity helps them to understand God's activity in the world as Father, Son and Holy Spirit
- God's Unity and Trinity are important as they are part of the teaching of the Bible and the Church.

Main points

The meaning of believing in God as Unity and Trinity

Christians believe there is only one God (God's Unity) who is in the world in three persons (the Holy Trinity). Believing in one God is called monotheism. Christians believe that God is One because everything in the universe shows it was made by one God.

When Christians speak of God as one, they call this God's substance. When Christians talk about God at work in the world they call it the three persons of God:

- The Father who created everything.
- The Son who showed what God is like and saved people from sin.
- The Holy Spirit who brings the presence of God into people's lives.

Christians only worship one God. The Trinity is a Unity. This is sometimes explained by symbols such as the shamrock.

Why it is important for Christians to believe in God's Unity

- The belief that God is one is the first of the Ten Commandments.
- Jesus said that worshipping one God is the greatest commandment.
- Belief in one God is the teaching of the Catholic Church (the Magisterium) in the Creeds and the Catechism.
- Christians believe that God is omnipotent, and only if God is a Unity can God be all-powerful.

Why it is important for Christians to believe in God as the Trinity

- The Trinity helps Christians understand the different ways that God has shown his presence in the world.
- The Bible shows the Trinity when at the baptism of Jesus the Father speaks, the Son is baptised and the Spirit descends in the form of a dove.
- Belief in the Trinity is a part of the Apostolic Tradition, and Christians must believe the teachings of the apostles.
- Belief in God as Trinity is the teaching of the Church through the Creeds and the Catechism.

Evaluation questions

You may be required to argue for and against it being important to believe in the Trinity to be a Christian/Catholic.

1. To argue for it being important, you can use the reasons why the Trinity is important listed in the main points above.
2. People who argue against could use such reasons as:

- If you believe in God's Unity that's enough, as even the Catechism says the Trinity is a mystery.
- If you love God and love your neighbour, you are a Christian whatever you think about the Trinity.
- If people follow the teachings of Jesus and go to Mass, it does not matter whether they believe in the Trinity or not.

Topic 10.1.2 The meaning, and importance for Christians, of believing in God as the Father

Main points

The meaning of believing in God as the Father

- Believing that God is the Father means that Christians should have a father–child relationship with God.
- It also shows that God has a relationship of love and care with his creation.
- In the 'Our Father', Christians learn that God provides daily bread and protection from evil simply because he is 'our Father'.
- Because God is the Father, Christians can turn to him when they are in need.

The importance for Christians of believing in God as the Father

- Jesus called God his Father and told his disciples to call God, Father. The teachings of Jesus are the basis of the Christian faith.
- The Creeds and the Catechism teach Catholics to call God their Father.
- If God had not been our Father, he would not have sent Jesus to explain how Christians should live and to save people from their sins.
- Believing in God as Father allows Christians to have a personal relationship with God.

Key points

- Believing in God as Father means that Christians can have a relationship with God like they can with a human father. It also means that God will love, care and provide for them.
- This is important for Catholics because it is the teaching of the Bible, Jesus and the Church. It is also important as it gives Christians God's love and salvation.

Evaluation questions

You may be required to argue for and against God being our Father.

1. To argue for, you could use the bullets from meaning and/or the bullets from importance in the main points above.

2. People who argue against, use such reasons as:
   - No good father would allow his children to experience evil and suffering.
   - No good father would not answer his children when they talk to him.
   - No good father would allow there to be different religions, so that his children do not know the right way to please him.

Topic 10.1.3 The meaning, and importance for Christians, of believing in God as Creator

Main points

The meaning of believing in God as the Creator

- God created the universe and all the things in it, so life has a meaning and purpose given to it by God.
- God created the universe out of nothing so he is all-powerful and is the cause of all life.
- As God has created the universe, the universe must be good.
- God created human beings in his image, so humans are special.

The importance for Christians of believing in God as the Creator

Believing in God as Creator is important because it shows:

- God's omnipotence – only an all-powerful God could create the universe.
- That the universe is not an accident. It was created by God, who is good, for a good purpose.
- That life is sacred because God created it and what God creates must be holy, so we need to treat creation carefully and with respect.
- God's love for humans. God created the world for humans and gave them their purpose in living.

Topic 10.1.4 The meaning, and importance for Christians, of believing that Jesus is the Son of God

Main points

The meaning of believing that Jesus is the Son of God

- Jesus is God incarnated. This means Jesus is God on Earth living as a human being, so in Jesus humans can see the nature of God.
- As Son of God, Christians believe that Jesus was both fully human and fully divine.
- As God's Son, Jesus had God's powers on Earth, which explains why he was able to work miracles.
- As the Son of God, Jesus' death was a sacrifice for the sins of the world, bringing God's salvation and, by rising from the dead, God's Son also brought eternal life.

The importance for Christians of believing that Jesus is the Son of God

- Only the Son of God could bring salvation from sin and give people the chance to enter heaven.
- Believing in Jesus as the Son of God gives Christians the chance to see the love shown by God's Son, leading them to share God's love with their neighbours.
- Believing that Jesus is the Son of God is a teaching of the Creeds and the Catechism of the Catholic Church.
- Believing that Jesus is the Son of God is important because only God's Son could institute the Mass which brings Christ into lives today.

Key points

Christian belief in Jesus as the Son of God means that Jesus was both man and God. He was conceived by the Holy Spirit and was God on Earth. His example and teaching show Christians how God wants them to live.

It is important that Jesus is the Son of God because:

- it explains that there is a special relationship between God and Jesus
- his life shows what God is like
- his life and death bring salvation and eternal life.

Evaluation questions

You may be required to argue for and against Jesus being the Son of God.

1. To argue for, you could use such reasons as:
   - Only the Son of God could rise from the dead.
   - Only the Son of God could perform the miracles Jesus did.
   - It is the teaching of the Bible and the Church.

2. People who argue against would use such reasons as:
   - The miracles of Jesus could have natural explanations.
   - It is more reasonable to believe that Jesus was the son of Mary and Joseph rather than Mary and God.
   - The resurrection can be explained and, if Jesus did not rise from the dead, then he was just a prophet.

Topic 10.1.5 The meaning, and importance for Christians, of believing in the Holy Spirit

Main points

The meaning of believing in the Holy Spirit

- The Holy Spirit is the means by which God communicates with humans, bringing God's presence into the world.
- The Holy Spirit inspired the Bible so that its writings reveal the nature and will of God.
- The Holy Spirit is how God helps the Church to keep the Apostolic Tradition and to give true teaching in the Magisterium.
- The Holy Spirit brings God's love and strength to Christians today.

The importance for Christians of believing in the Holy Spirit

- It is the third person of the Trinity and is God's presence in the world.
- Through baptism and reconciliation, it removes people's sin, allowing them to have eternal life.
- It inspires the teachings of the Church so the teachings of the Church should be obeyed as if they were the teachings of God.
- Its gifts enable Christians to live lives full of love, joy and peace, helping Christians live the lives Jesus wants them to live.

Evaluation questions

You may be required to argue for and against the Holy Spirit being important/active today.

1. To argue for, you could use the last bullet point in 'The meaning of believing in the Holy Spirit' and the last two bullet points in 'The importance for Christians of believing in the Holy Spirit', in the main points above.

2. People who argue against could use such reasons as:
   - If the Holy Spirit were active, all Christians would believe the same thing.
   - If the Holy Spirit were active, Christians would be full of peace and joy and they are not.
   - If the Holy Spirit were active, Christians would be living as Jesus wants them to live and many do not.

Topic 10.1.6 The meaning and importance of Christian beliefs about salvation from sin

Main points

The meaning of Christian beliefs about salvation from sin

- Sin is an action that breaks God's law and makes it difficult to be in contact with God because sin separates a person from God.
- Salvation means being saved from sin.
- The death of Jesus was the sacrifice needed to bring salvation from sin. So Jesus is the saviour of the world because he brought forgiveness and eternal life.
- Catholics believe that today, salvation comes through the Church and is brought about by receiving the sacraments and leading a Christian life.

The importance of Christian beliefs about salvation from sin

- Without salvation, a person's sins will send them to hell or purgatory after death.
- It is the only way that Christians can have eternal life with God.
- It was the reason why God became man. Salvation from sin was the purpose of the life, death and resurrection of Jesus.
- It is the reason why the sacraments of baptism, reconciliation, confirmation, healing and the Mass are so important.

Key points

Christians believe sin is what separates people from God and people who die with unforgiven sins will not go to heaven. They also believe that the sacrifice of Jesus brought salvation from sin, that is forgiveness and the promise of eternal life.

Catholics believe that salvation is important because it:

- saves people from hell and leads to eternal life with God
- was the purpose of the death of Jesus
- explains why we have the sacraments
- gives Christians a reason to live a holy life.

Evaluation questions

You may be required to argue for and against people needing to be saved from sin.

1. To argue for, you could use the first three bullets from 'The importance of Christian beliefs about salvation from sin' in the main points above.
2. Those who argue against would use such reasons as:
   - A loving God would not send his children to purgatory or hell.

- A loving, omnipotent God would not set a price for sin which involved making his Son die for the sins of the world, and if there is no price for sin, there is no need for salvation.
- Most people today do not think of themselves as sinful and cannot see why they need salvation.

Topic 10.1.7 The meaning and importance of loving God and how love of God affects Christians' lives

[handwritten margin notes: worship prayer, vocation = talents + abilities, obedience = using a Christian life, Evangelism = sharing the love of God with others.]

Main points

The meaning of loving God

Catholics show their love of God by worshipping him through:

- going to weekly Mass and praying every day
- taking the other sacraments of the Church
- following the Christian life as shown in the teachings of the Church
- using their talents and abilities in the service of God.

The importance of loving God

- Jesus said that loving God is the greatest commandment. Christians believe Jesus is God's Son therefore following his teachings helps them to gain eternal life.
- By loving God, Christians are living the life God wants.
- Loving God is a way for Christians to thank God for his love. God showed his love by sacrificing his Son to bring humans eternal life.
- The Church teaches in the Catechism that all believers should love God, as this is the basis of the Christian life.

How love of God affects Christians' lives

- Using their abilities and talents as God intends so that others benefit from them will affect a Christian's choice of career, marriage partner, use of money, etc.
- Showing respect towards God's creations will affect a Christian's life because they will have to make sure that the Earth and all the creatures on it are cared for.
- Following the rules set by God (the Ten Commandments and the Sermon on the Mount) is bound to have a big effect on a Christian's life (see Topics 10.4.5–10.4.9, pages 124–129).
- Following their calling from God (vocation) will have a huge effect on a Christian's life if they are called to the priesthood, the religious life, or service to the poor.

Evaluation questions

Advice on answering evaluation questions is after Topic 10.1.8 on page 78.

Topic 10.1.8 The meaning and importance of Christian teachings on the love of others

Main points

Mark 12:29–31

Jesus says that the second commandment is to love your neighbour as you love yourself. This means that a Christian's love for their neighbours:

- needs to be as strong as it is for themselves
- is second only to love of God himself
- is what God wants from Christians.

This Christian teaching is important because:

- It is a commandment from Jesus.
- By loving their neighbour Christians are doing God's will.
- It is not easy to do, but can lead to eternal life.

The Parable of the Good Samaritan – Luke 10:25–37

When asked who is your neighbour, Jesus told this parable: 'A Jew was travelling from Jerusalem to Jericho when he was attacked by robbers. Two important Jewish people ignored him, but a Samaritan (a race and religion who hated Jews) stopped and helped the injured man.' This parable means that:

- Christians need to show love to everyone
- loving your neighbours can make the difference between life and death
- loving your neighbour is what God wants.

This parable is important because:

- It is the teaching of Jesus.
- It shows Christians that loving your neighbour is not easy (the good people had good reasons for not helping), but it is what Christians have to do.
- It explains that your neighbour is anyone needing help, whatever their race or religion.

The Parable of the Sheep and the Goats – Matthew 25:31–46

Jesus told a story about the final judgement when, like a shepherd, he will separate people into sheep and goats. The sheep will be those who fed Jesus when he was hungry, gave him drink when he was thirsty, took him in when he was a stranger, clothed him when he needed clothes, looked after him when he was sick, visited him when he was in prison, and so they will go to heaven. The goats will be those who did none of these things for other people, so they will go to hell. This parable means that:

- Christians need to show love to everyone in need, because anyone in need could be Jesus
- by showing love for others Christians are showing love for God
- God will judge people on their actions, how they treat others.

This parable is important because it explains that:

- by showing love for others, Christians are showing love for God
- loving others means caring for those people who are hungry, thirsty, strangers, short of clothes, sick or in prison
- showing love to those who are suffering is rewarded by eternal life with God in heaven.

Evaluation questions

You may be asked to argue about whether love of neighbour is more important than love of God

1. To argue that it is more important, you could use such reasons as the three bullets on the meaning of the Sheep and the Goats, and the last bullet from the importance of the Sheep and the Goats in the main points.

2. People who disagree would use the reasons from 'The importance of loving God' in Topic 10.1.7 on page 76.

Topic 10.1.9 How love of God is expressed in the life of a religious community

Main points

Carmelite nuns are a mainly contemplative religious community who spend their lives in prayer and study. They show their love for God in the following ways:

- The nuns take the evangelical counsels (vows of poverty, chastity and obedience) to show their complete love of God.
- The nuns follow the Carmelite Rule, meaning that they:
  - meditate day and night on the Word of the Lord
  - celebrate the Eucharist every day
  - do manual work.

Clearly, to follow this rule, they must show great love for God.

- The nuns spend almost twelve hours a day in prayer, worship and contemplation of God.
- The nuns live away from the world trying to come closer to God.

Key points

Carmelite nuns show their love of God by:

- separating themselves from the world
- taking the evangelical counsels
- spending most of their lives in prayer and worship including daily Mass, and following the Carmelite Rule.

Evaluation questions

You may be asked to argue for and against joining a religious community as the best way of loving God.

1. To argue for, you could use the main points above for how Carmelites show their love for God.

2. Those who disagree may use such reasons as:
   - It cannot be what God wants because if everyone took the evangelical counsels, the human race would die out.
   - It is easy to pray at home each day and go to Mass once a week to show your love for God.
   - It is easier to love your neighbour outside a religious community because you come in contact with more people; and this is one way of loving God.

Topic 10.1.10 How love of others is expressed in the life of a religious community

Key points

The Missionaries of Charity are a religious community founded by Mother Teresa. They express their love of others by taking an extra vow to help the poorest of the poor and in their daily work of caring for the dying left on the streets of slums and caring for orphans, AIDS victims and lepers.

Main points

The Missionaries of Charity were founded by Mother Teresa in 1950. They express their love for others in the following ways:

- As well as taking the evangelical counsels (vows of poverty, chastity and obedience), they also vow to serve the poorest of the poor.
- For about twelve hours a day, the nuns and monks love others by working in the centres run by the order.
- Some centres are for the abandoned and dying of all castes and religions, to help them die with dignity, surrounded by God's love.
- The Missionaries also run orphanages, AIDS hospices, and care for lepers, refugees and victims of floods, epidemics and famine in order to share God's love with others.

Evaluation questions

You may be asked to argue for and against it being easier to love your neighbour in a religious community.

1. To argue for, you could use the main points above.

2. To argue against, you could use such reasons as:
   - In ordinary life you have opportunities to love your neighbour all the time not just when the religious community gives you time for it.

- Loving your neighbour means helping anyone who needs your help which you can do whether in a religious community or not.
- In a religious community, you have to follow the rules which could make you pray and meditate rather than love your neighbour.

Topic 10.1.11 How a Christian church shows love of God and love of others in a local area

Main points

Love of God in a local area (parish)

A Catholic church shows love of God by:

- Providing worship so that people can show their love of God in the celebration of Mass.
- Keeping the Blessed Sacrament in the tabernacle so people can show their love of God by adoring the Body of Christ.
- Offering the sacraments so that people can show their love of God through baptism, First Confession and Communion, confessions, confirmation and marriage.
- Giving regular Bible readings and homilies explaining those readings to the people so they can learn more about God and how to show their love for him.

Love of others in a local area (parish)

A Catholic church shows love of others in a local area by:

- Making sure that a Catholic grows up surrounded by people who not only share the same beliefs but also love them as brothers and sisters in Christ.
- Supporting the local Catholic primary and secondary schools, providing children's liturgies, classes in First Confession and Communion and Confirmation to help parents to keep their baptismal promises.
- Providing social facilities such as youth clubs, uniformed organisations, mother and toddler groups.
- Providing help for the needy through such groups as the St Vincent de Paul Society (SVP), CAFOD, lunch clubs for the elderly, and so on.

> ## Key points
>
> - A Catholic church shows love of God by being a place of worship of God and by providing the Mass and the sacraments.
> - A Catholic church shows love of others by helping parents raise their children as good Catholics, by helping the needy through SVP and CAFOD groups and by providing social facilities.

- run food banks to feed the hungry
- support refugees to welcome the stranger
- Building water wells to help the thirsty
- provide shelter to clothe the naked
- Being Prison Chaplains to visit the Prisoners
- Giving hospice care to visit the sick and dying.

Evaluation questions

You may be asked to argue for and against the church doing enough to show their love of others.

1. To argue for, you could use the main points in 'Love of others in a local area (parish)' above.

2. To argue against, you could use such reasons as:
   - There are always some people in need who are not helped.

- Some age groups may feel their needs are not catered for.
- Most church activities are aimed at Catholics who are active in the parish.

Section 10.2 Community and tradition

KEY WORDS FOR SECTION 10.2

Anglican Churches	Churches that are in communion with the Church of England
Apostolic	the belief that the Church can only be understood in the light of the apostles
Bishops	priests specially chosen by the Pope who are responsible for all the churches in a diocese
Catholic	universal or worldwide
Celibacy	living without engaging in any sexual activity
Holy	of, or relating to, God, sacred
Laity	all the people of the Church who are not chosen to be bishops, priests or deacons
Magisterium	the Pope and the bishops interpreting the Bible and tradition for Roman Catholics today
Nonconformist Churches	Protestant Christians separated from the Church of England
Ordination	making someone a priest, bishop or deacon by the sacrament of holy orders
Orthodox Churches	national Churches which are in the union with the Patriarch of Constantinople (e.g. the Russian Orthodox Church)
Papacy	the office of the Pope

Topic 10.2.1 The meaning, and importance for Catholics, of the Church as the means to faith and salvation

Main points

When Catholics say Church, with a capital C, they mean everyone who is a member of the Church.

What does 'the Church as the means to faith' mean?

- It is through the Church that people come to believe in Christianity so it is the means to faith.
- The Apostles were taught by Jesus and this teaching has been passed on to the Church through the Apostolic Succession. This means that people can learn the true faith from the Church.
- Catholics believe that only the Pope and the bishops can teach the true faith through the Magisterium of the Church. So it is only through the Church that the true faith can be found.
- Catholics learn to have faith in God through the actions of the Church such as preparation for: baptism, First Confession and First Communion, and confirmation.
- Catholics learn more about their faith through the readings and homily in Mass.
- Catholics learn more about, and are strengthened in, their faith through the Church's celebration of the sacraments.

Why the Church as the means to faith is important for Catholics

It is important because:

- If the Church is the means to faith, then it teaches the 'one true faith', handed down from the Apostles.
- The faith of the Church brings salvation and eternal life in heaven.
- Local parish churches provide a place where people can learn about the Catholic faith and become believers.
- People need something to help them believe and become members of the Church.
- The Church, through the sacraments, priests and lay people, provides people with the support and strength they need to believe and become good Catholics.

Key points

- The Church is the means to faith for Catholics because the Church has kept the faith of the Apostles and teaches it through worship and the sacraments. It is important to know the true faith and to be guided into it by the teaching and support of the Church.
- The Church is the way to salvation because the faith it teaches and the sacraments given by the Church bring forgiveness and then salvation from sin and death.

What does 'the Church as the means to salvation' mean?

Salvation means being saved from sin through the sacrifice of Christ (see Topic 10.1.6, page 75). The Church is the means to salvation because it provides:

- The sacrament of baptism which washes away original sin and makes a person a member of the Church.
- The sacrament of reconciliation where, if a person truly repents of their sins and determines to live a new life, their sins can be forgiven.
- The penitential rite of the Mass which gives people a chance to confess their sins and receive absolution, which forgives their sins.
- The sacrament of confirmation which makes a person a full member of the Church and gives the gifts of the Holy Spirit to help them on their way to salvation.
- The sacrament of the anointing of the sick where the final absolution and the food for the journey to heaven is the means to salvation and eternal life in heaven.

Why the Church as the means to salvation is important for Catholics

It is important because:

- Without salvation, a person's sins stop them from having close contact with God and send them to hell or purgatory after death.
- It is the only way that people can have eternal life with God.
- It gives Catholics a clear route to salvation. If they take part in the sacraments and follow the teachings of the Church, they will be saved.
- It shows that salvation is a continual process, rather than happening just once at baptism.
- Life is a journey to salvation and the Church gives Catholics chances to get back on the right path through the Mass and the sacraments of reconciliation and anointing.

Evaluation questions

You may be asked to argue for and against the Church being the only means to salvation.

1. To argue for, you could use the bullets from 'What does "the Church as the means to salvation" mean?' in the main points above.

2. People who argue against could use such reasons as:
   - Salvation can be gained through reading and believing the Bible.
   - Some Protestants believe salvation comes through a personal relationship with Jesus.
   - If the Church is the only means to salvation, then only Christians can go to heaven which goes against God being a God of love.

Topic 10.2.2 The meaning, and importance for Catholics, of the Church as the Body of Christ

Main points

What does 'the Church as the Body of Christ' mean?
- All Christians carry on Christ's work on Earth.
- The work of Christ on Earth did not finish with the Ascension; Jesus lives on through the Church, which is his body on Earth.
- Through baptism, Christians become part of the Church, and so part of the Body of Christ, which means they are united with each other and Christ.
- All Catholics receive the Body of Christ during Mass, which joins them with all the other Christians around the world receiving the sacrament.

Why the Church as the Body of Christ is important for Catholics
- This is how the Church is described in the New Testament and the Catechism.
- It explains the importance of the Mass. By sharing the consecrated host at communion, Catholics share in the Body of Christ.
- It shows how Christians can continue the helping and teaching work of Jesus today because they are the Body of Christ on Earth.
- It shows how Christians can perform different tasks and yet be a unity. There can be different talents and tasks (just as the body has different limbs and organs) and yet the Church remains a unity because all are working together as the Body of Christ.

Key points

Catholics believe that the Church is the Body of Christ on Earth because the Church carries on the work of Jesus on Earth, and is one body even though it has lots of different parts. This is important because:

- it is what the New Testament says
- it explains the importance of the Mass
- it shows how Christ is still active in the world.

Evaluation questions

You may be asked to argue for and against whether the Church should be called the Body of Christ.

1. To argue for, you should use the bullets from 'What does "the Church as the Body of Christ" mean?' in the main points above.
2. To argue against, you could use such reasons as:
   - The Christian Church is divided (e.g. Protestants and Catholics) whereas a body is united.
- Most Church members do not behave like Christ, which they should if they were carrying on his work.
- The Church does not appear to be Christ's body because it is rich but he was poor, it has power and political influence, but Christ rejected power and influence.

Topic 10.2.3 The meaning, and importance for Catholics, of the Church as the communion of saints

Key points

- The communion of saints means that Christians on Earth and Christians in heaven are in contact with each other and share their gifts and prayers with each other.
- This is important because it means that Catholics on Earth can ask the saints in heaven for help and Catholics in purgatory can be helped by the prayers of Catholics on Earth.

Main points

Saints are not just the official saints recognised by the Church, but are all faithful Christians.

What does 'the communion of saints' mean?

- Death does not separate Christians. All members of the Church are joined together: those on Earth, those in purgatory and those in heaven.
- Christians on Earth can offer prayers through the official saints, as they are in heaven rather than in purgatory.
- Catholics can pray for the dead as they are still part of the communion of saints. This means that Christians on Earth can pray for their dead relatives and friends in purgatory.
- Christians on Earth can have comfort and support from the prayers of dead Christians.

Why the Church as the communion of saints is important for Catholics

- It is the teaching of the Creeds and the Catechism that are the basis of Christian faith and in which all Catholics should believe.
- It gives Catholics direct contact with the official saints allowing Catholics to have help, comfort and support from great Christians of the past.
- It allows prayers to be offered for the dead so that those in purgatory can ascend to heaven and those in heaven can pray for those on Earth.
- It means that all Christians are equally important; all are joined and can pray for one another. No one Christian is more important than another.

Evaluation questions

You may be asked to argue for and against the communion of saints making sense today.

1. To argue for, you could use the bullets from 'What does "the communion of saints" mean?' in the main points above.

2. People who argue against could use such reasons as:

- It is hard to believe in heaven when science seems to show there is nowhere for heaven to exist.
- It is hard to believe that all the millions of people who have lived are in one place spending eternity praying.
- It is hard to believe that what happens to people after death can be changed by people still alive.

Topic 10.2.4 Why the Bible has authority and importance for Catholics

Main points

Why the Bible has authority for Catholics
Catholics believe the Bible has authority because it:
- is inspired by the Holy Spirit and so is holy and gives the truth which Catholics should accept and follow
- reveals God; they believe that God speaks through both the Old Testament and New Testament
- contains God's laws on how to behave, such as the Ten Commandments: these rules help people live as God wants them to live
- contains the teachings of Jesus on how to live the Christian life.

Why the Bible is important for Catholics
- The Bible records the teaching of Jesus which shows Christians what to believe, how to live and how to make decisions.
- The Bible records the life, death and resurrection of Jesus which is the basis of the Christian faith.
- The Bible contains the Ten Commandments which are God's basic guidelines on how to live.
- The Bible reveals what God is like and what he does for Christians.

Key points
- The Bible has authority because it is inspired by God and contains the teachings that come from God.
- The Bible is important for Catholics because it reveals God, contains God's commands on how Christians should behave, and shows Christians what Jesus did on Earth.

Evaluation questions
You may be asked to argue for and against everyone obeying the moral guidance/teachings of the Bible.

1. To argue for, you could use the first, third and fourth bullet points from 'Why the Bible has authority for Catholics' and the first and third bullets from 'Why the Bible is important for Catholics' in the main points above.

2. To argue against you could use such reasons as:
- The Bible was written thousands of years ago and so has no relevance to modern life.
- The Bible is a Christian book; you cannot expect Muslims, Hindus and atheists to follow it.
- The Bible's teachings on things like equal rights for women and homosexuals are no longer acceptable.

Topic 10.2.7 The meaning and importance of Protestant beliefs about the authority of the Church

- Within the Protestant Churches, the Church leads and guides and has authority on Church organisation; however, the Bible is the only true source of authority and salvation.
- These beliefs are important because they explain why there are different Protestant Churches with different beliefs, and why the Protestant Churches broke away from Rome.

Main points

The main Protestant beliefs about the authority of the Church

- The Bible can be understood by anyone if they have faith, and is the only authority, so the Church does not have the authority to interpret the Bible for Christians.
- Everyone is of equal value, therefore only decisions agreed to by all the members of the Church can have authority. For this reason Protestant Churches are ruled democratically and vote on issues.
- Any Church guidance is not a command, and so can be interpreted by members using their understanding of the Bible.
- The Church has the authority to decide on Church organisation, but salvation comes through the Bible alone.

Why these beliefs are important

- They explain why there are so many different Protestant Churches (e.g. Anglican Churches, Noncomformist Churches). If salvation depends on what people think the Bible means, those who disagree will set up new Churches.
- They show why the Protestant Churches cannot accept the authority of the Pope.
- They explain why there are different attitudes to the sacraments among Protestant Christians (most believe baptism and communion are the only sacraments, but Quakers and the Salvation Army have no sacraments).
- They explain why there are so many differences between Protestant Churches because there is no agreed Church authority.

Evaluation questions

You may be asked to argue for and against the Protestant attitude to the Church being better than the Catholic attitude.

1. To argue for, you could use the first three bullets from 'The main Protestant beliefs about the authority of the Church' in the main points above.

2. To argue against, you could use the bullets from 'The importance of the Magisterium for Catholics' in Topic 10.2.6, page 93, and/or the bullets from 'The importance of Apostolic Tradition' and 'The importance of the Apostolic Succession' in Topic 10.2.5, page 92.

Topic 10.2.8 The role and importance of the Pope and bishops in the Catholic Church

Main points

The role of the Pope in the Catholic Church

- To lead the worldwide Church, and make sure it is cared for.
- To organise the Magisterium and make sure it is kept up to date.
- To appoint and ordain new cardinals and bishops, and make sure their teaching is correct.
- To give guidance to Catholics about current issues (e.g. world poverty, community cohesion).

The importance of the Pope in the Catholic Church

The Pope is important for Catholics because:

- He is responsible for the beliefs and teachings of the Catholic Church.
- He is the successor of St Peter who passes on the true teachings of Christ to Catholics.
- He is the Head of the Church who appoints and ordains cardinals and bishops.
- He gives guidance and inspiration to Catholics.

The role of bishops in the Catholic Church

- To look after the needs of all the priests and laity in their diocese.
- To be responsible for all the priests in their diocese and make sure they are carrying out their roles properly.
- To be responsible for appointing, ordaining and disciplining the priests and deacons in their diocese.
- To act as the link between parishes and the Vatican, allowing the Pope to be in contact with the whole Church.

The importance of bishops in the Catholic Church

- Bishops are responsible, with the Pope, for the beliefs and teachings of the Church.
- The Cardinals, who elect the Pope, are chosen from bishops.
- Only bishops can ordain priests.
- Bishops make sure their diocese is following the faith of the Church and can correct and discipline any priest who teaches or acts incorrectly.

Key points

- The Pope is the Head of the Catholic Church who appoints and ordains cardinals and bishops and makes sure that they teach the true faith and give guidance to Catholics on current issues.
- The Pope is important because he is the Head of the Church, the successor of St Peter and the supreme authority for Catholics.
- Bishops are in charge of a diocese and must make sure the priests and people are well looked after and are taught the true faith.
- Bishops are important because only they can ordain priests. They make sure a diocese has the true faith and they help with the Magisterium.

Evaluation questions

You may be asked to argue for and against the Pope being the best person to decide what Christians should believe.

1. To argue for, you could use the reasons for the importance of the Pope in the main points above.

2. To argue against, you could use the first and last bullets from 'The importance of bishops' in the main points on page 95 and main points on the Magisterium (Topic 10.2.6, page 93) to emphasise that bishops are involved in deciding what Catholics should believe. Or you could use the bullets from 'The main Protestant beliefs about the authority of the Church' (Topic 10.2.7, page 94).

You may be asked to argue for and against the idea that all Christians should follow the guidance of the Pope.

1. To argue for, you could use the reasons for the importance of the Pope in the main points above.

2. To argue against, you could use the bullets from 'The main Protestant beliefs about the authority of the Church' (Topic 10.2.7, page 94).

Pope Benedict XVI performing a blessing during the canonisation mass in St Peter's Square in Rome, Italy, 12 October 2008.

Topic 10.2.9 The role and importance of the priest in the local parish

Main points

The role of the priest in the local parish
- To lead daily Mass and special occasion liturgies.
- To teach the people of the parish about the faith.
- To administer the sacraments and ensure that people are prepared fully for the sacraments.
- To look after the people within the parish, providing advice and counselling.

The importance of the priest in the local parish
Priests are important because they:
- fulfil the role of Jesus in the Mass and transubstantiate the bread and wine
- make sure the people are cared for, and the church runs smoothly
- give the people of the parish the sacraments which give them salvation and life in heaven
- can give advice on matters of faith and personal problems in order to help people
- help people with the important stages of their life – baptism, confirmation, marriage, funerals.

Evaluation questions

You may be asked to argue for and against every parish needing a priest.

1. To argue for, you could use the reasons for the importance of the priest in the main points above.
2. People who disagree could use such reasons as:
   - Lay ministers can administer the bread and wine which could have been consecrated by one priest for many parishes.
   - Lay people can baptise and conduct funerals, so a parish would only need a priest to visit occasionally for marriages, confirmations, etc.
   - Lay people can make sure the people are cared for and that the church runs smoothly.

Topic 10.2.10 Why Christians have different attitudes to the celibacy of the clergy

Key points

Catholic priests have to be celibate in order to copy what Jesus did, maintain tradition and be able to give their whole life to the Church. Other Christians allow their priests and ministers to marry as they feel there are many advantages to allowing priests to marry should they want to.

Main points

Why Catholics believe the clergy (priests) must be celibate

- It is tradition handed down from St Paul.
- Jesus was celibate and priests should follow his example.
- It allows priests to be completely devoted to God and have the time for their parishioners.
- Unmarried priests are free to deal with the needs of their parish without being distracted by a family.

Why other Christians allow priests to marry

- St Peter was married (Jesus healed Peter's mother-in-law).
- Married priests are better at recognising and dealing with married people's problems.
- Married priests were allowed in the early Church until celibacy became the norm.
- Non-Catholic Churches do not have a shortage of priests, but the Catholic Church in Europe does, perhaps because many men are put off joining the celibate priesthood.

Evaluation questions

You may be asked to argue for and against celibate priests being better than married priests.

1. To argue for, you should use the last three bullets from 'Why Catholics believe the clergy (priests) must be celibate' in the main points above.

2. To argue against, you could use the following arguments:
   - Married priests are better at recognising and dealing with married people's problems.
   - Married priests are more in touch with real life than celibate priests.
   - If they have a family, married priests will have a better understanding of the needs of Catholic schools.

Topic 10.2.11 The role and importance of the Virgin Mary for Catholics

Main points

The role of the Virgin Mary for Catholics

- For many Catholics, Mary's main role is to act as an intercessor. Prayers are said to Mary to ask for her prayers because of her special relationship with God.
- Mary is a role model who shows Christians how to live a good Christian life because she obeyed God's plan for her.
- Mary shows how to live a pure life. She was conceived without sin (Immaculate Conception) and remained a pure virgin throughout her life.
- Mary shows how to love Jesus. She loved her son and was with him right to the end, even sharing in his sufferings on the cross.

Why the Virgin Mary is important for Catholics

Mary is important for Catholics because:

- She had an immaculate conception. This means that Jesus was totally sinless because his mother was born without original sin and his father was God.
- If Mary had not obeyed God, Jesus would not have been born, and without his birth, there would be no Christianity and no salvation.
- The Virgin Birth means Mary gave birth to God and so she is 'the Mother of God'. As the Mother of God, Mary must be the most important human being ever to have lived.
- At the end of her life, she was taken up to heaven instead of dying (the Assumption of the Blessed Virgin Mary), so she did not suffer death like everyone else.
- In heaven, she is able to pray for the souls of Christians on Earth, so she can make the prayers of Catholics more effective and give them more chance of God's help.

Key points

- Catholics believe that the role of the Virgin Mary is to help their prayers to be accepted by God. She also acts as a role model to show Catholics how to live good lives, how to love Christ and how to be obedient to God.
- The Virgin Mary is important because she was totally obedient to God; she was the Mother of God, making sure Christianity began. She was taken up to heaven instead of dying and she can pray for the souls of Christians on Earth.

Evaluation questions

You may be asked to argue for and against the Virgin Mary being too important in the Catholic Church.

1. To argue for, you could use such Protestant reasons as:
   - Every Catholic church has a statue of the Virgin Mary, but Jesus should be the only object of worship.
   - Catholics offer prayers through the Virgin Mary, but the Bible says prayers should only be offered through Jesus.

- The belief in the Immaculate Conception and Assumption make Mary appear semi-divine, but they are not referred to in the Bible.

2. To argue against, you could use the reasons why the Virgin Mary is important for Catholics in the main points above.

SECTION 10.2 TEST

SECTION 10.2: Community and tradition

Answer both questions.

1. a) What is the Magisterium? (2 marks)

   b) Do you think that priests should be able to marry?
   Give two reasons for your point of view. (4 marks)

   c) Explain why it is important for Catholics to believe in the communion
   of saints. (8 marks)

   d) 'The Catholic Church is the only way to salvation.'

   (i) Do you agree? Give reasons for your opinion. (3 marks)

   (ii) Give reasons why some people may disagree with you. (3 marks)

   In your answer, you should refer to Christianity.

   (Total: 20 marks)

2. a) What are Nonconformist Churches? (2 marks)

   b) Do you think bishops are important?
   Give two reasons for your point of view. (4 marks)

   c) Explain why the priest is important for the local parish. (8 marks)

   d) 'The Bible is not relevant to people's lives today.'

   (i) Do you agree? Give reasons for your opinion. (3 marks)

   (ii) Give reasons why some people may disagree with you. (3 marks)

   In your answer you should refer to Christianity.

   (Total: 20 marks)

You should now use the mark scheme in Appendix 1, page 135, to mark your answers, and the self-help tables in Appendix 1, pages 136–137, to see how you can improve your performance. If you need more help with the mark scheme for these questions, go to www.hoddereducation.co.uk/catholicchristianity

Section 10.3 Worship and celebration

KEY WORDS FOR SECTION 10.3	
Absolution	through the action of the priest, God grants pardon and peace
Chrism	the oil used in baptism, confirmation and ordination
Commemoration	the belief that the Eucharist is simply a remembrance of the Last Supper
Contrition	sorrow for the sin committed and deciding not to sin again
Holy Week	the week before Easter Sunday
Liturgy of the Eucharist	the re-enactment of the Last Supper during which the bread and wine are transubstantiated
Liturgy of the word	the Bible readings in the second part of the Mass
Penance	an action to show your contrition
Penitential rite	the confession and absolution at the beginning of Mass
Rite of communion	receiving the body and blood of Jesus
Sacrament	an outward sign through which invisible grace is given to a person by Jesus
Transubstantiation	the belief that the bread and wine become the body and blood of Jesus

Topic 10.3.1 The meaning and importance of the sacrament of baptism

Main points

Sacraments are outward signs and symbols that an inward gift from God has been given.

The meaning of the sacrament of baptism

- Baptism comes from a Greek word meaning to dip, bathe or wash. In baptism, the old life is washed away and a new one is entered.
- At baptism a person becomes part of the Christian Church and so the baptised person can be called a Christian and is joined in faith with other Christians.
- Baptism is the first of the sacraments marking the beginning of the sacramental life which is essential for Catholics.
- In infant baptism the original sin with which the child is born is washed away, leaving the baptised person free of sin.

The importance of baptism

- The Catechism teaches that baptism is the basis of the Christian life and, without it, a person cannot receive the other sacraments.
- Through baptism, a person becomes a full member of the Church and is helped by the Church to begin a new life in the Holy Spirit and grow in faith.
- Baptism washes away original sin so that the baptised can achieve salvation.
- The Catechism says that baptism is necessary for salvation, and without salvation one cannot enter heaven.

Evaluation questions

You could be asked to argue for and against baptism being the most important sacrament.

1. To argue for, you could use the reasons for the importance of baptism in the main points above.

2. To argue against, you could use such reasons as:
   - Holy orders are more important because without priests there can be no sacraments.
   - The Mass is more important because it brings Christ into the lives of Catholics every week.
   - Reconciliation is more important because it forgives the sins you commit after baptism.

Topic 10.3.2 The meaning and importance of the sacrament of confirmation

Main points

The meaning of the sacrament of confirmation

- The sacrament of confirmation is the final sacrament of initiation and means that the person has fully joined the Catholic Church.
- The sacrament gives grace which is needed in order to live a Christian life and so eventually receive salvation.
- Confirmation joins people more closely to the Church so that they learn to live in the way the Church teaches.
- By retaking the baptismal vows for themselves, Catholics make a public declaration of their faith.

The importance of confirmation

- Confirmation makes the person a full member of the Church.
- Only those who are confirmed can take on lay ministries.
- Part of confirmation is the gift of the Holy Spirit which gives strength to develop faith and live the Christian life.
- In baptism, promises were made by the person's parents and godparents, while in confirmation it is the individual's own choice to declare his or her belief.

Key points

When a person is old enough to make their own decisions they are expected to renew their baptismal vows in the sacrament of confirmation. Confirmation is important because it gives the gifts of grace and the Holy Spirit which completes the sacraments of initiation and makes the person a full member of the Church.

Evaluation questions

You could be asked to argue for and against not needing to be confirmed to be a member of the Church and get to heaven.

1. To argue for, you could use the bullet points in 'The importance of baptism' in Topic 10.3.1, page 104.

2. To argue against, you could use the reasons in 'The importance of confirmation' in the main points above.

Topic 10.3.3 The meaning and importance of the sacrament of reconciliation

Key points

Catholics believe that the sacrament of reconciliation forgives a person's sins and brings them into a closer relationship with God. The sacrament is also important because it is a Precept of the Church that it is essential to receive the sacrament.

Main points

The meaning of the sacrament of reconciliation

- The sacrament of reconciliation (confession/penance) allows someone to recognise that they have separated themselves from God and that they need God's forgiveness for their sins and his help not to commit sins again.
- The sacrament gives grace to avoid sins that lead away from salvation.
- As part of the sacrament, advice is given about how to overcome temptation, and follow the path to salvation.
- Receiving the sacrament of reconciliation at least once a year is one of the Precepts of the Church (rules that Catholics are expected to follow), and Catholics believe that following the Church's Precepts will lead to salvation.

The importance of reconciliation

Reconciliation is important for Catholics because:

- It gives the opportunity for the penitent to strengthen their relationship with God.
- The gift of grace given during the sacrament makes it easier for the penitent to live a Christian life.
- Attending the sacrament allows the penitent to be reconciled with the community as well as with God.
- The sacrament brings the forgiveness of serious sins necessary to receive the Eucharist, receive salvation and enter heaven.

Evaluation questions

You could be asked to argue for and against the sacrament of reconciliation being needed today.

1. To argue for the sacrament still being needed, you could use the reasons for the importance of reconciliation in the main points above.

2. To argue that it is no longer necessary, you could use such reasons as:
   - God loves us and will forgive our sins if we ask him directly without having to go through a priest.
   - The Penitential Rite in the Mass forgives Catholics their sins every week.
   - Many Catholics only go to confession once a year, at Lent, so it cannot be needed very much.

Topic 10.3.4 The meaning and importance of the sacrament of anointing of the sick

Main points

The meaning of the sacrament of anointing of the sick

- The sacrament of anointing of the sick is a strengthening sacrament, for those in danger of death.
- The sacrament is a gift of grace that helps a person deal with their illness.
- The sacrament can be used to prepare very ill people for death.
- The sacrament reminds the sick person and the community that the Church today can still heal like Jesus and the disciples in the early Church.

The importance of anointing of the sick

- The sacrament gives grace, spiritual strength and healing to the person, and so is a very supportive sacrament.
- The sacrament makes all Christians holy, not only the person receiving the sacrament.
- The sacrament is a reassuring one by showing the love of the parish for the sick person.
- The sacrament allows the person's sins to be forgiven, so they can enter heaven.

Key points

The sacrament of the anointing of the sick gives seriously ill people the strength to face grave illness and death. It is important because it gives spiritual help as the person receives the Holy Spirit and grace from God which forgives their sins and strengthens their faith. The sacrament also joins the recipient with the Christian community and with the suffering of Christ.

Evaluation questions

You may be asked to argue for and against the sacrament of anointing being needed today.

1. To argue for its being needed, you should use the reasons for the importance of the sacrament in the main points above.

2. To argue against, you could use such reasons as:
   - It is just as effective if all the parish prays for whoever is sick.

- It is hard to believe that a loving God would stop Catholics from going to heaven just because they had not had the 'last rites'.
- The shortage of priests means that many sick people do not get the full sacrament, just a visit and prayers from a lay minister with pre-consecrated bread and wine.

Topic 10.3.5 The nature and importance of the Mass

Key points

The Mass is a re-enactment of the Last Supper and a celebration of the resurrection of Jesus. It is important for Catholics because it is a chance for them to meet as a community in the presence of God, to give thanks to God, to remember the sacrifice of Jesus, to receive the Eucharist and to receive the grace of God to help them grow in faith.

Main points

The nature of the Mass

- The Mass is a re-enactment of the Last Supper and a celebration of the resurrection of Jesus.
- The first part of the Mass, the penitential rite, makes Catholics aware that they are sinners and need the forgiveness of God on a regular basis.
- Next is the liturgy of the word with Bible readings and usually a homily explaining the readings and relating them to Catholic life today.
- The liturgy of the Eucharist follows when the Eucharistic Prayer re-enacts the Last Supper and changes the bread and wine by transubstantiation into the body and blood of Christ. This is given to the people in the rite of communion.
- In the final part of the Mass, Catholics give thanks and receive a blessing to help them in the week ahead.

The importance of the Mass

- During Mass, bread and wine are turned into the body and blood of Christ, so Jesus is really present during Mass.
- It is a celebration of the resurrection, reminding all Catholics that there is eternal life, and that one day they too will be able to receive eternal life.
- Receiving the body and blood of Christ joins Catholics with Jesus, and so brings them closer to salvation.
- The first Precept of the Church says Catholics should attend Mass every Sunday and on holy days.
- Attending Mass was commanded by Jesus at the Last Supper, and the Catechism says it is a sin knowingly to miss Mass on Sundays and holy days of obligation.

Evaluation questions

You may be asked to argue for and against Sunday Mass being the most important Catholic celebration.

1. To argue for, you could use the reasons for the importance of Mass in the main points above.

2. To argue against, you could use such reasons as:
   - For a priest and his family, ordination would be the most important celebration because it is a total change of life.
   - For many Catholic families, First Confession and Communion is the most important celebration because it sets their children off on the Catholic life.
   - For many couples, marriage is the most important celebration as it is the beginning of a life-long relationship and the start of a new family.

Topic 10.3.6 The meaning of the Eucharist in other Christian traditions

Main points

The Eastern Orthodox Church

In the Eastern Orthodox Church, the Eucharist:

- is a sacrament where the bread and wine become the body and blood of Jesus by a holy mystery
- is part of the Divine Liturgy during which heaven comes to Earth in the bread and wine
- fills the people with the presence of Christ and with every grace and blessing from God
- follows the actions and words of Jesus during the Last Supper and remembers the sacrifice of Christ on the cross.

Nonconformist Protestant Churches

Most Nonconformist Protestants call the Eucharist Holy Communion which:

- is a commemoration of the Last Supper, where the bread and wine are symbols which do not change
- fills Christians with the presence of Christ and with every grace and blessing from God
- brings unity as the worshippers share the one Body of Christ
- is a reminder of the Last Supper and the crucifixion of Christ.

The Church of England

There are different attitudes to the Eucharist in the Church of England.

- Those who believe in priests and seven sacraments have similar beliefs to Catholics.
- Those who believe in ministers and two sacraments (baptism and Holy Communion) have Nonconformist Protestant beliefs about the Eucharist.

The Salvation Army and Quakers

The Salvation Army and Quakers have no Eucharist because they believe:

- Jesus is the only priest
- worship should be direct contact with God without symbols
- they can lead holy lives without the use of sacraments.

Key points

Christians understand the Eucharist in different ways and refer to it using different names. Eastern Orthodox Christians believe the bread and wine changes to the body and blood of Jesus by a holy mystery; most Protestants believe the bread and wine do not change, but that during the celebration of Holy Communion Jesus becomes spiritually present.

Evaluation questions

You may be asked to argue for and against the Eucharist being important for Christians.

1. To argue for, you should use the first and second bullet points from 'The importance of the Mass' in Topic 10.3.5, page 108, the second point from 'The Eastern Orthodox Church' and the second point from 'Nonconformist Protestant Churches' in the main points on page 109.

2. To argue against, you could give the reasons why Quakers and the Salvation Army do not celebrate the Eucharist, in the main points on page 109.

You may be asked to argue for and against the bread and wine becoming the body and blood of Jesus.

1. To argue for, you could use such reasons as:
   - Transubstantiation is a teaching of the Catechism and so must be believed by Catholics.
   - At the Last Supper Jesus said, 'This is my body', 'This is my blood'.
   - By becoming the body and blood of Jesus, the Eucharist enables Christ to enter the lives of believers in a full way.

2. To argue against, you could use such reasons as:
   - The Protestant Churches do not believe the bread and wine change.
   - There is no other evidence that elements can have their substance changed.
   - The bread and wine do not look any different after transubstantiation, so why should people believe they have changed?

Topic 10.3.7 Why Catholic churches have certain features

Main points

The altar is the centre of attention because the priest offers Mass on the altar as a symbol of Christ offering himself as a sacrifice to God on the cross. It is positioned so that the priest can face the congregation as he celebrates the Mass. On or near the altar are candles whose light represents the belief that Jesus is the light of the world.

The tabernacle has a place of honour, usually next to the altar because it contains the consecrated hosts of the Blessed Sacrament reserved there for distribution to the sick. Catholics believe Jesus is really present in the Blessed Sacrament and show their reverence for Jesus by genuflecting towards the tabernacle whenever they walk past it.

The baptismal font containing holy water is usually at the entrance (the back) of the church to remind Catholics that baptism is what makes a person a member of the Church.

The confessional is a small room set aside for the sacrament of reconciliation. By penance and absolution, Catholics are reconciled to God and to each other.

The lectern is a book-stand from which the liturgy of the word takes place showing the belief that faith and truth come from the Bible (the readings) and the teaching of the Church (the homily).

All Catholic churches have statues of Mary and some of the saints. They are visual aids to help the congregation in their prayer. Catholics do not pray to the statues.

Key points

A Catholic church has many different features that show important Catholic beliefs such as transubstantiation, the new life brought by baptism, the importance of the Bible and the teachings of the Church.

Evaluation questions

You may be asked to argue for and against the idea that Catholic churches need the features they have in order to have the right worship or the right beliefs.

1. To argue for you could use the reasons for having the altar, the tabernacle, the lectern and the baptismal font.

2. To argue against, you could use such reasons as:
   - You could use any sort of flat surface to celebrate Mass, and Catholic beliefs about transubstantiation would not be affected.

- The readings and the homily could be given by a priest sitting among the congregation and it would not affect the beliefs or worship.
- Baptism could take place outside the church in a stream/river/pond and the worship and teachings would not be affected

(Of course you do need a tabernacle for unused elements if you believe in transubstantiation.)

Topic 10.3.8 The meaning and importance of Christmas

Key points

Christmas is important for Christians because without the birth of Jesus there would be no Christianity and no salvation from sin. Christmas is an opportunity to remember God's gift to humanity and to worship God accordingly.

Main points

The meaning of Christmas

- Christmas is the celebration of the incarnation (the belief that God took human form in Jesus).
- Catholics believe that through the incarnation (which led to the life, death and the resurrection of Jesus) it became possible for humans to have a full relationship with God and to go to heaven after death.
- Christmas tells Christians that God showed his love by sending his son to show humans what God is like and to teach them how to live.
- Christmas is a time of hope and peace, when Catholics pray for the coming of the Kingdom of God.

The importance of Christmas

- Without the birth of Jesus Christ, there would be no Christianity.
- Through the incarnation, God began the salvation of the world so making it possible for humans to go to heaven after death.
- Through celebrating the birth of Christ, Catholics recognise that he was born not only to teach and work miracles, but also to suffer and die to save humans from sin.
- The celebrations such as Christmas Mass and the papal blessing *Urbi et Orbi* remind Catholics they are part of a worldwide community.
- It is a time to celebrate families, reflecting that Jesus was born into a human family.

Evaluation questions

You may be asked to argue for and against Christmas only being celebrated by Christians.

1. To argue for, you could use any of the reasons on the meaning of Christmas in the main points above.
2. To argue against, you could use such reasons as:
   - Non-Christians celebrating Christmas might make them think about Christianity.
   - Christmas cards, presents and parties spread the joy of Christmas to everyone.
   - Joining in all religious celebrations helps to promote community cohesion.

Often Christmas and Easter will be joined together in a question. Advice on evaluation questions such as these are after Topic 10.3.11 on page 115.

Topic 10.3.9 The meaning and importance of Lent

Main points

The meaning of Lent

- On Ash Wednesday Catholics go to church for a special Penitential Mass. As a sign of their penitence they have a cross of ashes smeared on their forehead by the priest to remind them that during Lent they should pray more, fast more and give more to charity.
- Catholics try to give up something to make them into better people and show devotion to God.
- Catholics try to pray more and strengthen their faith by acts of mercy such as visiting the sick and housebound.
- There are special meetings (often with other Christian Churches) to think about Easter and what it means to be a Christian today.

The importance of Lent

Lent is important for Catholics because:

- It is a time when Catholics concentrate on improving their Christian lives.
- It is a chance to think about the teachings of Jesus and what they mean for today.
- The readings during Mass are based on the later part of Jesus' life and these help Catholics work out what they need to do in their lives in order to achieve salvation.
- It is a time when Catholics try to increase their faith through extra prayer, study, fasting and giving to charity.

> ## Key points
>
> Lent is forty days of preparation for Easter beginning with Ash Wednesday. It reflects the time Jesus spent in the desert preparing spiritually for his ministry. Lent is important because during Lent, Catholics try to change their lives so that they can enter the kingdom of heaven. They give up things, pray more often and meet with other Christians to think about what Jesus did and what it means to be a Christian today.

Evaluation questions

You may be asked to argue for and against the practices of Lent bringing Catholics closer to God.

1. To argue for, you could use the last three bullets of 'The meaning of Lent' in the main points above.

2. To argue against, you could use such reasons as:
   - Fasting makes you irritable and think about food rather than God.
   - Thinking about what it means to be a Christian today in discussion groups with other Christian Churches can make you doubt things rather than bringing you closer to God.
   - Praying more and helping people more is likely to give you spiritual pride rather than bring you closer to God.

You may be asked to argue for and against Lent being important for Catholics.

1. To argue for, you could use the reasons from 'The importance of Lent' in the main points above.

2. To argue against you could use such reasons as:
   - Attending Mass is important but Lent does not really make much difference to a Catholic's life.
   - Lent reminds Catholics of the Passion of Christ, which Catholics can be reminded of in many different ways.
   - For many Catholics, Ash Wednesday is the only bit of Lent they observe.

Topic 10.3.10 The meaning and importance of Holy Week

Key points

Holy Week is the last week of Lent. It is a week when Catholics re-enact and remember the final week of Jesus' life. It is important because Catholics use this week to try to make up for their sins and try to make themselves spiritually pure.

Main points

The meaning of Holy Week

- Holy Week begins on Palm Sunday, includes Maundy Thursday and Good Friday and ends on Holy Saturday.
- During Holy Week Catholics remember the final week of the life of Jesus, recalling what Jesus did and taught from his entrance into Jerusalem on Palm Sunday to his death on Good Friday.
- During Holy Week there are special liturgies such as the Stations of the Cross, and during the Easter Triduum there are re-enactments of the Last Supper on Maundy Thursday and the arrest, trial and crucifixion of Jesus on Good Friday.
- Holy Week is a time of reflection and prayer on the sufferings and death of Jesus which saved Catholics from sin and allowed entry to heaven.

The importance of Holy Week

Holy Week is important for Catholics because it:

- reminds Catholics that they need to serve one another and put themselves last as well as be public witnesses to their faith
- should inspire Catholics to think about their role in the world, especially when they are asked to stand up for others in the cause of justice and peace
- reminds Catholics of the suffering Jesus experienced, which helps them to face their suffering
- reminds them of the salvation brought by Jesus. It was the death of Jesus that overcame sin, and during Holy Week Catholics try to do things to make up for their sinfulness (reparation).

Evaluation questions

You could be asked to argue for and against Holy Week being important.

1. To argue for, you could use the reasons for the importance of Holy Week in the main points above.
2. To argue against, you could use such reasons as:
   - It is more important for Catholics to live out their Christianity every week of the year rather than just one.
   - It is more important for Catholics to attend Mass every Sunday so they are reminded of the sacrifice and Last Supper of Jesus every week.
   - It is more important to show your love of God by loving your neighbour rather than spending a week in church.

Topic 10.3.11 The meaning and importance of Easter

Main points

The meaning of Easter

- Easter is the most important Christian celebration because the resurrection of Christ proves his identity. If Jesus rose from the dead, he must have been both human and divine (the two natures taught in the Creeds and the Catechism).
- The resurrection is the final part of salvation because through the resurrection, forgiveness of sins is assured and people can be restored to God.
- The resurrection proves that death has been overcome and assures Christians that they will have eternal life.
- Easter gives Catholics a chance to think about the mysteries of their faith and deepen their personal belief.

The importance of Easter

Easter is important for Catholics because:

- It celebrates the resurrection of Jesus which proves that Jesus is God, since no one but God could rise from the dead.
- It proves that there is life after death. If Jesus rose from the dead, his faithful followers will have life after death in heaven.
- It celebrates Jesus' victory over death and evil, which is why new Catholics are often baptised on Easter Day.
- It proves that what Jesus said about his death and resurrection was true, therefore Christians can believe the other things he said.
- It proves that Jesus is still alive and working in his Church.

> ## Key points
>
> Easter Day celebrates the resurrection of Jesus: Jesus rising from the dead on the Sunday after Good Friday. Catholics celebrate with the Easter Vigil when they renew their baptismal vows. It is important because it proves Jesus is the Son of God and gives Christians the hope of eternal life.

Evaluation questions

You may be asked to argue for and against Christmas being the most important festival.

1. To argue for, you could use the reasons for the importance of Christmas (Topic 10.3.8 on page 112).
2. To argue against, you could use the reasons for the importance of Easter in the main points above.

You may be asked to argue for and against Easter only being celebrated by Christians.

1. To argue for, you could use any of the reasons on the meaning of Easter in the main points above.
2. To argue against, you could use such reasons as:
   - Non-Christians celebrating Easter might make them think about Christianity.
   - Easter eggs and hot cross buns spread the joy of Easter to everyone.
   - Joining in all religious celebrations helps to promote community cohesion.

How to answer questions on Section 10.3

You should already know the basics about how to answer questions from Section 10.1, page 82, but here is an answer to a whole question on Section 10.3 with a commentary to help you.

Question a)
What is absolution? (2 marks)

Answer

When your sins are forgiven.

> One mark for a partially correct answer.

Answer

Through the action of the priest, God grants pardon and peace.

> Two marks for a correct definition.

Question b)
Do you think Catholics should go to Mass every Sunday? Give TWO reasons for your point of view.
(4 marks)

Answer

Yes because it is a Precept of the Church ...

> One mark for a reason.

... that Catholics should attend Mass every Sunday and on holy days.

> Two marks because the reason is developed.

Also, attending Mass was commanded by Jesus at the Last Supper ...

> Three marks because a second reason is given.

... and the Catechism says it is a sin knowingly to miss Mass on Sundays and holy days of obligation.

> Four marks because the second reason is developed.

> Total = four marks.

Question c)
Explain why the Eucharist has different meanings in other Christian traditions. (8 marks)

Answer

In most Protestant Churches, the Eucharist is only a commemoration because they do not believe in transubstantiation.

> LEVEL 1: two marks for one reason expressed in basic English.

As the bread and wine are not changed, Protestants believe that Christ is spiritually present and so fills the people with his presence.

> LEVEL 2: by giving a second reason, the answer goes up to level 2 and because the answer is written in clear English it would gain four marks

Protestants do not believe the Eucharist can re-enact the Last Supper and sacrifice of Jesus as the Mass does, and so they believe it is just a reminder of the Last Supper and the crucifixion of Christ.

> LEVEL 3: by adding another reason the answer moves up to level 3 and because the answer is written in a clear style of English with some use of specialist vocabulary (Protestant, commemoration, transubstantiation, spiritually present, sacrifice, Mass, Last Supper, crucifixion) it would gain six marks.

The Salvation Army and Quakers have no Eucharist because they believe Jesus is the only priest and that worship should be direct contact with God without symbols.

> LEVEL 4: by adding a further reason for the second attitude, the answer moves up to level 4 and because it is written in a clear and correct style of English with extra specialist vocabulary (Salvation Army, Quakers, Jesus, priest, symbols) it would gain eight marks – full marks.

Question d)

'Easter is the most important Christian festival.'

(i) Do you agree? Give reasons for your opinion.   (3 marks)
(ii) Give reasons why some people may disagree with you.   (3 marks)

In your answer, you should refer to Christianity.

Answer

(i) I disagree because Christmas is the celebration of the incarnation (the belief that God took human form in Jesus) and without the birth of Jesus Christ, there would be no Christianity.

> One mark for a reason for own opinion.

Through the incarnation, God began the salvation of the world so making it possible for humans to go to heaven after death.

> Another reason is given so it moves up to two marks.

Through celebrating the birth of Christ, Catholics recognise that he was born not only to teach and work miracles, but also to suffer and die to save humans from sin.

> The answer now gives another reason, so it moves up to three marks.

(ii) Some people might disagree with me because they think Easter is more important because it celebrates the resurrection of Jesus which proves that Jesus is God, since no one but God could rise from the dead.

> One mark for a reason why some people may disagree.

Easter proves that there is life after death. If Jesus rose from the dead, his faithful followers will have life after death in heaven.

> Another reason is given so it moves up to two marks.

Finally, Easter proves that what Jesus said about his death and resurrection was true, therefore Christians can believe the other things he said.

> The answer now gives another reason for the opinion, so it moves up to three marks.

> This answer to question d) can gain full marks because both parts refer to Christianity.

SECTION 10.3 TEST

SECTION 10.3: Worship and celebration

Answer both questions.

1. a) What is contrition? (2 marks)

   b) Do you think you need to be confirmed to be a good Catholic?
      Give two reasons for your point of view. (4 marks)

   c) Explain why Catholic churches have certain features. (8 marks)

   d) 'Only Christians should celebrate Christmas.'

      (i) Do you agree? Give reasons for your opinion. (3 marks)

      (ii) Give reasons why some people may disagree with you. (3 marks)

      In your answer you should refer to Christianity.

   (Total: 20 marks)

2. a) What is the penitential rite? (2 marks)

   b) Do you think Holy Week is important?
      Give two reasons for your point of view. (4 marks)

   c) Explain why the sacrament of anointing the sick is important for Catholics. (8 marks)

   d) 'Baptism is the most important sacrament.'

      (i) Do you agree? Give reasons for your opinion. (3 marks)

      (ii) Give reasons why some people may disagree with you. (3 marks)

      In your answer you should refer to Christianity.

   (Total: 20 marks)

You should now use the mark scheme in Appendix 1, page 135, to mark your answers, and the self-help tables in Appendix 1, pages 136–137, to see how you can improve your performance. If you need more help with the mark scheme for these questions, go to www.hoddereducation.co.uk/catholicchristianity

Section 10.4 Living the Christian life

KEY WORDS FOR SECTION 10.4

Active life	the life lived by religious orders who work in society as well as praying
Charity	voluntary giving to those in need
Contemplative life	the life of prayer and meditation lived by some religious orders
Displaying religion	making a show of your religion, e.g. by praying in the street
The evangelical counsels	the vows of poverty, chastity and obedience
Holy orders	the status of a priest, bishop or deacon
Hypocrite	a person who acts in a way that contradicts what they say
The Law of Moses	the laws God gave to Moses in the Old Testament
The monastic life	living as a monk or nun in a monastic community
Religious community	a religious order who live together as a group, e.g. the Benedictines
The Sermon on the Mount	Jesus' description of Christian living
Vocation	a call from God to lead the Christian life

Topic 10.4.1 The meaning of vocation and why it is important for Christians

Main points

The meaning of vocation

The word vocation means calling. Christians believe they have a calling from God to be followers of Jesus, to be members of the Church and to live their lives in the Christian way so that they enter heaven after death.

Christians often describe vocation as a call to discipleship. This means that all Christians are called for a special purpose in the same way that the Apostles were.

Vocation also means that all Christians must do what God calls them to do in the same way that Jesus did his Father's will. Therefore, all Christians must show their vocation by showing others the love of God, their faith in Jesus and the power of the Holy Spirit in their lives.

Why vocation is important for Christians

Vocation is important because:

- It shows all Christians are called to live a life of discipleship, just as the Apostles were.
- It shows that all Christians must do what God calls them to do if they want to achieve salvation. Vocation is a call from God and obeying it is doing God's will.
- By following a vocation, Christians are not only doing what God wants them to do, they are bringing more people to God by their example.
- By serving God through following a vocation a Christian will lead a holy life and work towards salvation.

Topic 10.4.2 How and why Christians show vocation in daily life and work

Main points

How Christians show vocation in daily life and work

- By choosing a caring profession such as being a doctor, nurse, carer, teacher, counsellor, or a person working for equal opportunities, they can show God's love.
- By marrying and bringing up children in a Christian family, which means the parents act as disciples through teaching the faith.
- By showing Christian love of neighbour in the way they treat other people.
- By being honest at work, giving a fair day's work to their employer, being fair to employees, and standing up for justice in the workplace.

Why Christians show vocation in daily life and work

- Vocation is about the whole of life and Christians need to serve God in all that they do.
- Christians believe that Jesus' final command to his disciples to go and 'baptise all nations' meant they should show their faith in all their actions and in what they say to others.
- Christian vocation is the call to love God and love one's neighbour in the whole of life as Jesus commanded his disciples in the greatest commandment.
- Christian vocation cannot be restricted to church or Sundays. The call to be a Christian must involve everything a Christian does.

Key points

- Christians show vocation in their daily life and work in many different ways. It can be by the job they choose, such as a doctor or a carer. Or it can be the way they treat people and live their lives.
- It is important for Christians to show their vocation in their daily life because vocation means serving God in everything you do.

Evaluation questions

You could be asked to argue for and against the need for Christians to show their vocation in their daily life and work.

1. To argue that they do, you could use the reasons from 'Why Christians show vocation in daily life and work' in the main points above.

2. To argue that they do not need to show their vocation, you could use such reasons as:
- Showing your vocation in your daily life and work can involve making a display of your religion which Jesus said is wrong.
- You can love God by praying and worshipping without showing your vocation at work.
- You can love your neighbour without anyone knowing it is because of your Christian vocation.

Topic 10.4.3 How and why some Christians show vocation by taking holy orders

Key points

- Some men receive a special vocation from God to take the sacrament of holy orders and devote their lives to God as deacons, priests or bishops.
- Holy orders means that a man has a vocation of discipleship and witness and he does this by serving the Church as an ordained minister.

Main points

How some Christians show vocation by taking holy orders

- By taking holy orders Christian men copy the work of the Apostles by giving up everything to follow Jesus.
- When men take holy orders they promise to serve just as Jesus served people.
- By taking holy orders men witness their faith to other people and show God's love to those who suffer.
- By taking holy orders men try to build the Kingdom of God by running parish communities.

Why some Christians show vocation by taking holy orders

Men take holy orders because:
- They have a special calling from God to devote their lives to his service through becoming priests.
- It is a calling that most priests could not ignore. If they tried to ignore God's call, it was so persistent that they had to accept it.
- It is the way in which they can 'share in the mission that Christ entrusted the apostles' (Catechism 1565).
- They want to serve God in the Church by celebrating the sacraments that give spiritual food and strength to the people.

Evaluation questions

You may be asked to argue for and against holy orders being the most important vocation.

1. To argue for, you could use the first two bullet points from 'How some Christians show vocation by taking holy orders' and the last two bullet points from 'Why some Christians show vocation by taking holy orders' in the main points above.

2. To argue against, you could use such reasons as:
- The most important vocation must be open to everyone and women cannot take holy orders.
- Jesus said loving God and loving your neighbour were the most important calls from God.
- Marrying and raising a Christian family are the most important vocations as they guarantee the survival of Christianity.

Topic 10.4.4 How and why some Christians are involved in working for social and community cohesion

Main points

How some Christians are involved in working for social and community cohesion

- Many Christians work for social and community cohesion as individuals by having friends from different faiths and ethnic groups, supporting community cohesion and opposing any racist or religious discrimination they meet.
- The Catholic Education Service (CES) works for social and community cohesion by making sure Catholic schools are open to all ethnic groups and teach about non-Christian faiths.
- Churches Together promotes community cohesion by bringing different ethnic groups together and setting up the Churches' Racial Justice Network.
- Some Christians form their own groups to take part in local activities with other faiths and minority groups to improve the quality of life in communities.

> ## Key points
>
> Individual Christians work for cohesion by making friends with people of different ethnic groups and religions. The Catholic Education Service does it by encouraging study of non-Christian religions. Churches Together encourages different ethnic groups to work together. Christians do this work to follow the teachings of the Bible and Jesus and because it is the teaching of the Church.

Why some Christians are involved in working for social and community cohesion

- In the Parable of the Good Samaritan, Jesus taught that Christians should love their neighbours of all races.
- St Peter was given a vision by God showing him that God accepts the worship of anyone who does right whatever their race.
- St Paul taught that as all humans come from Adam, all ethnic groups are equal to each other.
- The Catechism teaches that it is the duty of Catholics to work for social and community cohesion.

Evaluation questions

You could be asked to argue for and against the idea that Catholics do not do enough to promote community cohesion.

1. To argue for, you could use such reasons as:
   - Not all Catholics are involved in working for community cohesion.
   - Not all Catholic schools are following the community cohesion advice of the CES.
   - Some Catholics do not want to have anything to do with non-Catholic religions.

2. To argue against, you could use the reasons from 'How some Christians are involved in working for social and community cohesion' in the main points above.

You may be asked to argue for and against the idea that all Catholics should be involved in promoting community cohesion.

1. To argue for, you could use the reasons from 'Why some Christians are involved in working for community cohesion' in the main points above.

2. To argue against, you could use such reasons as:
   - If people are forced to co-operate, it might lead to fighting and hatred of different groups which is very unChristian.
   - It does not matter if different cultural communities follow their own ideas about society as long as they all follow British laws.
   - Community cohesion is not possible; the rich have different ideas from the poor, the workers from the employers, etc., so it is more important for Catholics to follow Jesus' command to love God and their neighbour.

Topic 10.4.5 How and why Christians use the Ten Commandments as a guide for living

Key points

- Christians use the Ten Commandments to help them worship one God, avoid swearing, honour their parents and live a good Christian life.
- Christians use the commandments as a guide for living because they are precise rules about how to respect God, how to behave and how to regard possessions.

The Ten Commandments

1. You shall worship God alone.
2. You shall not make idols nor worship them.
3. You shall not take God's name in vain.
4. Keep the Sabbath day holy by doing no work on it.
5. Honour your parents.
6. Do not kill.
7. Do not commit adultery.
8. Do not steal.
9. Do not tell lies.
10. Do not covet other people's possessions.

Main points

How Christians use the Ten Commandments as a guide for living

- Through their prayers and worship, Christians show that they are following the first three commandments.
- Many Christians do not swear; especially they do not swear using God's name.
- Catholics use the command to honour the Sabbath day as a reason for attending Mass every Sunday (Sunday became the Sabbath for Christians when Jesus rose from the dead on Sunday).
- Christians use: do not steal, do not kill, do not commit adultery, do not lie, do not desire other people's things, to help them make moral decisions.

Why Christians use the Ten Commandments as a guide for living

- The Ten Commandments are a precise list of rules from God on how Christians should behave.
- If Christians follow the first three commandments, they will be worshipping the one God of the Apostles' Creed.
- Following the last seven commandments will give Christians a good relationship with their neighbours.
- The commandments promote marriage and family life (respect for parents, no adultery, not desiring other people's partners).

Evaluation questions

You may be asked to argue for and against the Ten Commandments being the best guide for Christian living.

1. To argue for, you should use the reasons from 'Why Christians use the Ten Commandments as a guide for living' in the main points above.

2. To argue against, you could use the reasons why Christians use the teachings of the Sermon on the Mount on the re-interpretation of the Law of Moses (Topic 10.4.6, page 125) and on the Golden Rule (Topic 10.4.9, page 128) as a guide for living.

You may be asked to argue for and against the Ten Commandments being relevant/needed in the twenty-first century.

1. To argue that they are, you should use such reasons as:
   - Respect for parents, no adultery, not desiring other people's partners promotes family life.
   - Not stealing or lying makes life more civilised for everyone.
   - Not killing makes life safer for everyone.

2. To argue against, you could use such reasons as:
   - Worshipping God is not relevant to atheists and agnostics.
   - The Sabbath is the seventh day of the week (Saturday) and not working on a Saturday is not acceptable to many people today.
   - Not saying such things as 'Oh my God!' would be impossible for most people today.

Topic 10.4.6 How and why Christians use the teachings of the Sermon on the Mount on the re-interpretation of the Law of Moses as a guide for living

Main points

The main teachings of Jesus on how to live the Christian life are contained in the Sermon on the Mount in Matthew's Gospel. Jesus teaches his followers about the Law of Moses (Jewish teaching) and the commandments and how they should interpret them.

How Christians use the teachings as a guide for living

- Christians can be guided against anger by Jesus' teaching that to be angry with someone can lead to murder. Therefore, you must seek forgiveness and reconciliation.
- Married Christians may be guided by Jesus' teaching that lustful thoughts about someone other than your marriage partner are as bad as committing adultery.
- They may also be guided by his teaching that, although the Law of Moses allows divorce, if you re-marry after divorce you are committing adultery.
- Many Christians use Jesus' teachings about an eye for an eye to become pacifists.

Why Christians use the teachings as a guide for living

- This is the teaching of Jesus and has a lot more detail than the Ten Commandments, so Christians know exactly what to do.
- The Sermon on the Mount shows that the old Jewish ways have been fulfilled by the new law of Jesus.
- The Sermon on the Mount explains that the thoughts and feelings that people have are as important as their actions.
- If Jesus thought his disciples needed this teaching, it must also be needed by Christians today.

Key points

- Christians use the teachings of Jesus on the Law of Moses to decide how to react to such things as anger, lustful thoughts, divorce then re-marriage, making promises in the name of God, revenge and retaliation.
- Christians use the teachings as a guide for living because these come from Jesus and are a development of the less detailed laws of Moses.

Evaluation questions

You could be asked to argue for and against Christians never fighting.

1. To argue for, you could use such reasons as:
   - Jesus taught in his Sermon on the Mount that Christians should not resist evil and that if they are hit on the right cheek they should turn and offer the left.
   - Jesus also taught that Christians should love their enemies. It seems impossible to love someone you are fighting.

- Jesus also said you should pray for those who hate you, not fight them.

2. To argue against, you could use such reasons as:
   - It is the teaching of all the main Churches that Christians have the right to fight in just wars.
   - Jesus never condemned the soldiers he met.
   - Everyone has the right to defend themselves if they are attacked.

Topic 10.4.9 How and why Christians use the teachings of the Sermon on the Mount on judgement and the Golden Rule as a guide for living

Key points

- Christians use the teachings on judgement to help them in their personal relationships and to work out how they can be judged well by God. They use the Golden Rule as a simple guide to decide what is the right thing to do.
- Christians follow these teachings because they come from God's Son, Jesus, and they provide clear advice on how to live and gain eternal life.

Main points

The Golden Rule is, 'So in everything, do to others what you would have them do to you, for this sums up the Law and the Prophets' (Matthew 7:12).

How Christians use the teachings as a guide for living

- Jesus taught that if people judge someone, they must expect to be judged in the same way. So, before Christians criticise other people, they should think about whether they could also be criticised.
- Christians use the teaching on judgement to concentrate on trying to improve themselves rather than picking on the things that other people do wrong.
- Lots of rules are difficult to follow, so many Christians find it easy to follow the simple rule, 'treat other people as you would like to be treated'.
- Christians also use the Golden Rule to decide on major issues by trying to work out how they would want to be treated if they were involved in the issue.

Why Christians use the teachings as a guide for living

- Jesus, as God's Son, is the best person to show Christians when to judge.
- If Jesus gives a Golden Rule, it must be a rule worth using as a guide for living.
- If Christians are going to be judged by God, the teachings of Jesus on judgement must be worth using as a guide for living.
- The Catechism says that the Golden Rule helps Christians to work out how to behave in difficult situations.

Evaluation questions

You could be asked to argue for and against having the right to judge others.

1. To argue for having the right, you could use such reasons as:
   - Judgement is a natural thing and judging some people to be bad can stop you getting into trouble.
   - We have to make judgements in life, for example deciding who to have as a friend.
   - Magistrates and judges have to judge people to make society safe from criminals.

2. To argue against, you could use the first and second bullet points from 'How Christians use the teachings as a guide for living' and the first bullet from 'Why Christians use the teachings as a guide for living' in the main points on page 128.

You may be asked to argue for and against the Golden Rule being the best guide for living.

1. To argue for, you could use the third and fourth bullet points from 'How Christians use the teachings as a guide for living' and the second and fourth points from 'Why Christians use the teachings as a guide for living' in the main points on page 128.

2. To argue against, you could use such reasons as:
   - Some Christians think the Golden Rule is too vague and that God would not have given laws in the Bible if they were not to be followed.
   - Some Christians believe they should follow what all other Christians agree is the right way to behave, such as the Ten Commandments, rather than relying on their own ideas.
   - Some Christians think the Church knows better what Christians should do than the individual and so they follow the guidance of the Church.

Topic 10.4.10 How one Catholic organisation helps to relieve poverty and suffering in the United Kingdom

Main points

One of the main Catholic organisations that helps to relieve poverty and suffering in the UK is the St Vincent de Paul Society (SVP). Many parishes, schools, universities and hospitals have an SVP group which relieves poverty and suffering by:

- Regular visiting and personal care by the same people to help: families with difficulties, the lonely and/or bereaved, the depressed, the housebound.
- Organising holiday schemes for children from poor or broken homes, family carers, poor families, people with disabilities, etc. These lead to increased self-esteem and confidence.
- Organising furniture stores for unwanted furniture, which can be used when housing the homeless, etc.
- Organising housing associations to provide affordable housing for the homeless, overcrowded poor families, etc.
- Providing drop-in centres for lonely people to have an opportunity to socialise.

Evaluation questions

You may be asked to argue for and against whether Catholics are doing enough to relieve poverty and suffering in the UK.

1. To argue for, you could use the bullets from how one Catholic organisation helps relieve poverty and suffering in the UK, in the main points above.

2. To argue against, you could use such reasons as:
   - Not all Catholics are involved in working to relieve poverty and suffering.
   - Not all Catholic parishes have an SVP conference.
   - There is a lot of poverty and suffering which is not tackled by the SVP.

Topic 10.4.11 Why Catholic organisations help to relieve poverty and suffering in the United Kingdom

Main points

Catholic organisations help to relieve poverty and suffering in the UK because:

- Jesus said riches must be used for the help of others, especially the poor.
- Christianity teaches that all humans are equal, and that all the good things of the Earth have been given by God for people to use to help each other.
- In the Parable of the Sheep and the Goats people are sent to heaven because they fed the hungry, gave drink to the thirsty, clothed the naked and visited those in prison.
- Jesus did all he could to help the suffering and Christians should follow his example.
- Helping to relieve poverty and suffering is a way of loving your neighbour.
- The Church teaches that Catholics should relieve poverty and suffering, and Catholics should follow the teachings and advice of the Church.

Key points

Catholic organisations help to relieve poverty and suffering in the UK to try to follow:

- the teachings of Jesus in the Sermon on the Mount and in parables like the Sheep and the Goats
- the teachings of the Church that Christians should help the poor and suffering
- the example of Jesus who healed the suffering.

Evaluation questions

You could be asked to argue for and against the idea that it is more important for Catholics to love and worship God than spend time relieving poverty and suffering.

1. To argue for, you should use reasons from 'The importance of loving God' in Topic 10.1.7 on page 76.

2. To argue against, you should use the reasons from this topic in the main points above.

How to answer questions on Section 10.4

You should already know the basics about how to answer questions from Section 10.1, page 82, but here is an answer to a whole question on Section 10.4 with a commentary to help you.

Question a)
What is the monastic life? (2 marks)

Answer
Living in a monastery.

One mark for a partially correct answer.

Answer
Living as a monk or nun in a monastic community.

Two marks for a correct definition.

Question b)
Do you think the Golden Rule is a good guide for making decisions? Give TWO reasons for your point of view. (4 marks)

Answer
Yes because it is a guide for every situation ...

One mark for a reason.

... which is easy to use and following which will lead us to eternal life.

Two marks because the reason is developed.

Also, it is a teaching of Jesus ...

Three marks because a second reason is given.

... and Catholics believe that following the teachings of Jesus is the best way to live.

Four marks because the second reason is developed.

Total = four marks.

Question c)
Explain why Christians should show vocation in daily life and work. (8 marks)

Answer
Catholic Christians believe they should show their vocation in daily life and work because they believe vocation is about the whole of life.

LEVEL 1: two marks for a reason expressed in basic English.

Christian vocation is the call to love God and love one's neighbour in the whole of life as Jesus commanded his disciples in the greatest commandment.

LEVEL 2: by giving a second reason, the answer goes up to level 2 and because the answer is written in clear English it would gain four marks.

Even when they fall in love, Christians must still show their vocation by taking the sacrament of marriage and bringing up children in a Christian family through baptism, First Confession and Communion and going to Mass every Sunday.

LEVEL 3: by adding another reason the answer moves up to level 3 and because the answer is written in a clear style of English with some use of specialist vocabulary (love of God and neighbour, Jesus, disciples, greatest commandment, sacrament, baptism, First Confession and Communion, Mass) it would gain six marks.

Vocation is about the whole of life and Christians need to serve God in all that they do. So when they go to work, Christians should show their vocation by being honest at work, giving a fair day's work to their employer, being fair to employees, and standing up for justice in the workplace.

LEVEL 4: by adding a further reason, the answer moves up to level 4 and because it is written in a clear and correct style of English with extra specialist vocabulary (serve God, honest, fair day's work, standing up for justice) it would gain eight marks – full marks.

Question d)

'The government is better than religion at relieving poverty and suffering in the UK.'

(i) Do you agree? Give reasons for your opinion.   (3 marks)
(ii) Give reasons why some people may disagree with you.   (3 marks)

In your answer, you should refer to Christianity.

Answer

(i) I do agree because the government provides the National Health Service which spends billions of pounds a year in providing free treatment for all those suffering from illnesses.

> One mark for a personal opinion with a reason.

Also, the government provides social security for the poor so that everyone has the right to some income and housing no matter how poor they are and this too costs far more than religion could spend.

> Another reason is given so it moves up to two marks.

Finally, the government can raises taxes from the whole of UK society to provide relief for poverty and suffering whereas religion is dependent on people's spare cash, so the government must be better at relieving poverty and suffering.

> The answer now gives another reason for their opinion, so it moves up to three marks.

(ii) Some Christians might disagree with me because they think religious help like the SVP is much better because it provides love not just financial support.

> One mark for a reason why some people might disagree.

For example, the SVP provides regular visiting and personal care by the same people to help: families with difficulties, the lonely and/or bereaved, the depressed, the housebound. This requires Christian love which can never be given by the government.

> Another reason is given so it moves up to two marks.

One of the main causes of suffering for the old and widowed is loneliness. The SVP provides drop-in centres where caring Catholic Christians give such people an opportunity to meet and chat, receiving the sort of compassionate care the government can never provide.

> The answer now gives another reason for some people disagreeing, so it moves up to three marks.

> This answer to question d) can gain full marks because part (ii) refers to Christianity.

SECTION 10.4 TEST

SECTION 10.4: Living the Christian life

Answer both questions.

1. a) What are the evangelical counsels? (2 marks)

   b) Do you think Christians should love their enemies?
      Give two reasons for your point of view. (4 marks)

   c) Explain how some Christians are involved in working for social and
      community cohesion. (8 marks)

   d) 'Christians should never pray where people can see them.'

      (i) Do you agree? Give reasons for your opinion. (3 marks)
      (ii) Give reasons why some people may disagree with you. (3 marks)

      In your answer you should refer to Christianity.

   (Total: 20 marks)

2. a) What is the contemplative life? (2 marks)

   b) Do you think vocation is important for all Christians?
      Give two reasons for your point of view. (4 marks)

   c) Explain why some Christians show vocation by taking holy orders. (8 marks)

   d) 'The Ten Commandments are the best guide for Christian living.'

      (i) Do you agree? Give reasons for your opinion. (3 marks)
      (ii) Give reasons why some people may disagree with you. (3 marks)

      In your answer you should refer to Christianity.

   (Total: 20 marks)

You should now use the mark scheme in Appendix 1, page 135, to mark your
answers, and the self-help tables in Appendix 1, pages 136–137, to see how you
can improve your performance. If you need more help with the mark scheme for
these questions, go to www.hoddereducation.co.uk/catholicchristianity

Mark scheme for section tests

a) questions (2 marks)

Use the key words list on page 2 for Section 3.1, page 19 for Section 3.2, page 35 for Section 3.3, page 52 for Section 3.4, page 69 for Section 10.1, page 86 for Section 10.2, page 103 for Section 10.3, page 119 for Section 10.4. Award 2 marks for a correct answer.

b) questions (4 marks)

- A personal response with one brief reason award 1 mark.
- A personal response with two brief reasons award 2 marks.
- A personal response with one developed reason award 2 marks.
- For a personal response with two reasons with one developed award 3 marks.
- For a personal response with two developed reasons award 4 marks.

c) questions (8 marks)

- Level 1: For a brief reason in basic English award 2 marks.
- Level 2: For two brief reasons in basic English award 4 marks.
- Level 3: For three brief reasons written in a clear style with some specialist vocabulary award 5 or 6 marks depending on the Quality of Written Communication (QWC).
- Level 4: for four brief reasons written in a clear and correct style of English with a correct use of specialist vocabulary award 7 or 8 marks depending on the QWC.

d) questions (6 marks)

Part (i)
- One reason award 1 mark.
- Two reasons award 2 marks.
- Three reasons award 3 marks.

Part (ii)
- One reason award 1 mark.
- Two reasons award 2 marks.
- Three reasons award 3 marks.

How to improve your performance

When you have completed each test, copy and complete this table using your marks.

	Question 1	Question 2
1. How many marks did I get for question a)?		
2. How many marks did I get for question b)? If less than 4:		
• Did I forget to give reasons?		
• Did I forget to develop my reasons?		
3. How many marks did I get for question c)? If less than 8:		
• Did I forget to use specialist vocabulary?		
• Did I describe instead of explain?		
• Did I misunderstand the question?		
• Did I give too few reasons?		
• Did I forget about the Quality of Written Communication?		
4. How many marks did I get for question d)? If less than 6:		
• Did I forget to make one point of view be from one religion?		
• Did I forget to use information from the book?		
• Did I give too few reasons for part (i)?		
• Did I give too few reasons for part (ii)?		

Now use your completed table to complete a copy of this sheet which will show you what you need to do to improve:

HOW TO IMPROVE MY PERFORMANCE

Using the mark table, circle the targets that apply to you.

1. Question a)

Marks	Target
4 or more marks	Make sure I still know all the key words
3 or fewer marks	Learn the key words more thoroughly

2. Question b)

Marks	Target
Yes to bullet point 1	Remember to give reasons for my opinion
Yes to bullet point 2	Make sure I write developed reasons for my opinion

3. Question c)

Marks	Target
Yes to bullet point 1	Remember to use the key words in my part c) answers Learn and use specialist terms
Yes to bullet point 2	Practise understanding questions so that I explain why or how
Yes to bullet point 3	Make sure you read the question carefully and answer what it asks for, not what you want it to ask for
Yes to bullet point 4	Make sure to give four reasons
Yes to bullet point 5	Remember to take care with spelling and punctuation Remember not to use bullet points

4. Question d)

Marks	Target
Yes to bullet point 1	Make sure that either your own point of view or the one which disagrees with you is Catholic
Yes to bullet point 2	Make sure to use reasons from the revision guide
Yes to bullet point 3 or 4	Make sure to give three reasons for each part

How to deal with the exam paper

1. When you go into the exam hall and find your desk, your exam paper should be face up on the desk. Before you are allowed to open the paper, you can complete the front cover by:
   - writing your surname in the first top box
   - writing your first names in the adjoining box (if there is not enough room, write initials for those that will not fit)
   - writing your centre number (this will be on display in the hall) in the first box below
   - writing your personal exam number (you will receive this from your school before the exam) in the adjoining box.

   It is important that you get all of these completely correct, otherwise someone else may get your mark and grade!

2. When you are told to start, make a note of the time. You have 22 minutes per question (you could work on – part a) 2 minutes, part b) 4 minutes, part c) 10 minutes, part d) 6 minutes). You should try not to go beyond this as you will lose marks on Section 4 if you run out of time.

3. Start on Section 1 by choosing one of the questions, *either the whole of* question 1 (parts a, b, c, d) or *the whole of* question 2 (parts a, b, c, d). You should decide on which question to choose by whether you can do parts c) and d) as these are worth 14 marks of the 20 available.

4. Make sure you read the question carefully before you answer it and highlight key words such as *why, how, some, others, refer to Christianity.*

5. Make sure you put a line through the box beside the question you have chosen at the top of the first answer page. Your answers will be scanned and put onto a website, and the examiner will only be marking specific questions. If you do not indicate which question you have answered, your answer may not be marked.

6. If you run out of space, ask for a supplementary sheet of paper. The scanner does not pick up any writing outside the margins!

7. If you have any time left:
   - check that you have answered every part of each question
   - go through each answer to part c) checking the spelling and grammar and trying to add some extra specialist vocabulary, e.g. could you use any of the key words?
   - go through each part d) answer checking that you have three reasons for each point of view and adding reasons where necessary.